SO YOU ARE THE SUPERVISOR

Oliver W. Pittenger

ASQC Quality Press
American Society for Quality Control
310 West Wisconsin Avenue
Milwaukee, Wisconsin 53203

Published by

ASQC Quality Press
• Milwaukee •

So You Are The Supervisor

Oliver W. Pittenger

Copyright © 1986
by ASQC Quality Press.

All rights reserved. No part of this
book may be reproduced in any form or by
any means, electronic, mechanical, photocopying,
recording or otherwise, without the prior permission of
the publisher.

ISBN 0-87389-026-4

TABLE OF CONTENTS

Introduction 1
Lesson Plan Examples 7
Work Force 15
Leadership 27
Communication 35
Decision Making 45
Problem Solving 49
Motivation 55
Planning 69
Time Management 81
Organizing and the Organization 87
Delegation 109
Budgeting 115
Labor Relations 121
Reassessment 127
Bibliography 129
Index 135

Exercises

The Ideal Supervisor or Manager 20
Self-Examination 22
Leadership 27
One- and Two-Way Communication 37
Personal Two-Way Communication 40
Personal Motivation 57
Job Description 97
Conducting an Interview 100
Performance Review 102
Role Playing a Performance Review 103
Budgeting 118
Self-Examination (Reassessment) 127

Case Studies

Practicing Leadership Skills 32
Decision Making and Problem Solving 53
Employee Turnover or Some Other Problem? 63
Problem Employee 66
Do You Delegate? 112

INTRODUCTION

SO YOU ARE THE SUPERVISOR

SETTING THE STAGE

Lights, camera . . . material, director (leader), and the cast (students) are the elements needed to put together this course.

In trying to put the course together the focal point is on the director; the director is also called the trainer, guide, leader, instructor, or coach. This individual needs a special background to give the most to and get the most from the students. The leader should:

1. Be willing to guide the students in a respectful and honest manner. That is a respectful and honest feeling of self and others.
2. Be able to inform others about different experiences from an honest and trusting point of view.
3. Be able to guide small groups of students in different learning experiences with the primary objective of being positive in resolving individual problems.
4. Be able to express self in a positive, yet real-world approach to situations and problems.
5. Be able to allow for differing points of view in the classroom.
6. Be able to guide, coach, and lead students in discussions and problem-solving situations.
7. Have a philosophy that human resources come first. This is followed by tasks and remembering that without humans the tasks would not be completed.
8. Be able to provide an honest, fair, trusting, and consistent environment for learning.
9. Be able to learn with and from the students.
10. Be able to lead discussions and other activities in a nonsexist and nonracist manner.

Materials

The materials used in this course are just as important as the leader. Without the script (materials), the course would be difficult or impossible to conduct.

These materials are designed with the leader and students in mind. In order that the materials meet the needs of the students, the leader needs to be flexible in selecting the approach to meet each individual's goals and objectives. The leader can use all or just part of the suggestions supplied within this guide to develop the lesson plans, discussions, outlines, work sheets, overhead materials, and other activities. All these teaching aids can be individually created, but they need to meet the goals and objectives of the course.

The students have the flexibility to discuss situations and problems in a free and honest environment by using real-world exercises, case studies, and class discussions provided by their individual problems and situations. The students can develop an awareness of the real business world and self-confidence in their job performance skills. In this regard, these materials are appropriate for use by the beginner and the seasoned supervisor or manager alike.

Each lesson and chapter is designed to complete two basic objectives for both the leader and the students. The first objective is to build from life and classroom experiences. The second objective is to gain confidence in the individual basic skills of supervision and management through positive reinforcement from each exercise and chapter.

Course Description

This course is a discussion of the basic principles of supervision and management for quality, manufacturing, service, and other disciplines within any corporate structure. The handling of everyday problems and situations is discussed with emphasis upon individual needs.

This course deals with problems related to making individual appraisals, selecting employees, giving employee directions, handling personnel difficulties, training employees, and handling morale within a department you supervise. Leadership, communication, decision making, problem solving, motivation, and other related topics are also part of this course and material. This course uses class discussions, exercises, case studies, and other activities to reinforce decision-making and problem-solving techniques. This course uses personal experiences to add a more real-world atmosphere, but in a relaxed environment, for learning.

Getting Started

As the leader, the first activity will be for you to find out why the students are attending this course. The exercise to be used is simple, but it provides a learning tool for you and your students to use during the class.

The directions are:

1. Have the students list on paper their goals and objectives for taking the course and what they hope to gain by the experience. Be sure to have them include their name and date. Collect the papers.

2. Halfway through the course, return these papers to the students so they can determine if the class is meeting their goals and objectives. At this time the students are to evaluate the course. They can also change their goals and objectives, if need be. Again, collect the papers.

3. Do the same exercise in the last session of the course.

This will give you an indication of what items you need to revise or reinforce for future classes. The students will determine what is important to them — enabling them to exercise their right to make changes and giving them a sense of control over their lives.

Included are a set of lesson plans to assist you in guiding the students through this course in an effective manner.

LESSON PLANS

LESSON PLAN EXAMPLES

Lesson I. Introduction

Goal:
   To present the students with an outline of the course and materials to be used by discussing the topics in the materials.

Materials:
   "Setting the Stage" section
   Handouts:
      1. Course outline
      2. Course readings

How to:
   1. Introduce self.
   2. Have each student introduce herself or himself.
   3. Hand out resource information materials.
   4. Discuss the resource information materials.
   5. Discuss grading system and absenteeism.
   6. Discuss the type of course and what is expected of the group:
      a. Participation
      b. Group Work
      c. Exercises
   7. Have the students write their goals and objectives for the questions:
      a. "Why are you here?"
      b. "What do you want to achieve?"
      c. "What is most important to you that meets your needs and wants?"

Conclusion:
   1. Each student completes personal goals and objectives.
   2. Leader determines course direction for the group based on goals and objectives.

Assignment:
   1. Assign readings on the work force, pages 15-24.
   2. Complete the exercise "The Ideal Supervisor or Manager" on page 20.
   3. Complete the self-examination exercise on page 22.

Comments:

Lesson II. Work Force

Goal:
To examine the work force as a unit made up of individuals, not tasks.
To have the individuals participate in an open dialogue about the work force.

Materials:
Reading materials on work force

How to:
1. Review material in Lesson I.
2. Discuss answers to the questions:
   a. "Who is the work force?"
   b. "What is my role as a manager in the work force and work place?"
3. Discuss the results of the completed exercise.
4. Discuss the sexual harassment policy included in the materials.
5. Discuss the statement: "We develop attitudes and opinions about each other, but we really do not spend much time developing ourselves."
6. Have the students find out about themselves by completing the self-analysis exercise on page 22.
7. Discuss, in small groups, stress and our reactions to stress.

Conclusion:
1. Students will be exposed to the conditions in the work force that may be new to them.
2. Students will learn about themselves.
3. Students will have the opportunity to express their opinions about the work force and work place.

Assignment:
1. Read the unit on leadership, pages 25-34.
2. Complete the leadership exercise on page 27.
3. Read the case study on practicing leadership skills and complete the first step (i.e., answer the questions), page 32.

Comments:

Lesson III. Leadership

Goal:
To have the students become aware of their leadership and development skills by providing information and opportunities to them.

Materials:
Unit on leadership

How to:
1. Review Lesson II.
2. Ask if there are any questions about Lessons I and II.
3. Complete the leadership exercise on page 27, and review the exercise with the students.
4. Discuss leadership skills and styles.
5. Discuss leadership skills in meetings.
6. Exercise: Have the students develop a meeting by using the skills they are developing.
7. Discuss the meeting format presented in the materials and how to run an effective meeting.
8. Complete case study on leadership, page 32, and answer the questions in subgroups. Next discuss the case with the total group.
9. Discuss the summary of the leadership unit.

Conclusions:
1. Students are able to participate in groups.
2. Students use leadership skills in groups.
3. Students determine how groups work and function.

Assignment:
Read the section on communication, pages 35-44.

Comments:

Lesson IV. Communication

Goal:
To have students improve their communication skills.

Materials:
Unit on communication

How to:
1. Review Lesson III and answer any questions.
2. Ask for a volunteer and do the exercise on one-way communication, page 37.
3. With the same volunteer do the exercise on two-way communication, page 38.
4. Ask students to discuss what they learned from this communication exercise.
5. Ask students to discuss what they believe communication is.
6. Discuss the four most prominent types of communication within an organization.
7. Discuss the forms of communication.
8. Discuss giving instructions and orders.
9. Complete the exercise on personal two-way communication on page 40.

Conclusions:
1. Students improve their communication skills.
2. Students learn about other people in the group.

Assignment:
1. Read units on decision making and problem solving, pages 45-54.
2. Answer the questions about the case study on decision making and problem solving, page 53.

Comments:

Lesson V. Decision Making and Problem Solving

Goal:
To improve individual skills in making decisions and solving problems.

Materials:
Units on decision making and problem solving

How to:
1. Review Lesson IV and discuss any questions.
2. Discuss the process of decision making.
3. Discuss obstacles and overcoming the problems involved with good decision making.
4. Discuss how to problem solve.
5. Discuss task force information.
6. Complete the decision-making and problem-solving case study, page 53.
7. Discuss the results of the case.

Conclusion:
Provide information and experience in making decisions and solving problems.

Assignment:
1. Read the unit on motivation, pages 55-68.
2. Complete the exercise on personal motivation, page 57.
3. Complete the case studies on employee turnover and the problem employee, pages 63 and 66.

Comments:

Lesson VI. Motivation

Goal:
Discuss and determine attitudes, morale, motivation, and constructive criticism changes and problems.

Materials:
Unit on motivation

How to:
1. Review Lesson V and discuss any questions.
2. For the purpose of gathering feedback, discuss the goals and objectives written by each individual in the first session and have each student ask himself:
    a. Are my goals and objectives being met and how?
    b. Have my goals and objectives changed?
    c. How is the course progressing? (Negative and positive statements.)
    d. How can the course be improved?
3. Discuss misconceptions about motivation.
4. Discuss the merits of different theories by behavioral scientists.
5. Discuss motivational environments and the elements of motivation.
6. Discuss attitudes, behavior, morale, plus changes that may and can occur.
7. Discuss the case study on employee turnover.
8. Discuss disciplining employees.
9. Discuss the problem employee case study.
10. Discuss discipline problems and corrective actions.
11. Discuss constructive criticism.

Conclusions:
1. Goals and objectives are developed in the course by each student.
2. Inspire and create change in attitudes, morale, and motivations.
3. Positive group work experience.

Assignment:
Read units on planning and time management, pages 69-86.

Comments:

Lesson VII. Planning and Time Management

Goal:
To understand the importance of planning and time management.
To develop an outline with the final result in mind: the *plan*.
Learn how to organize for and develop effective results.

Materials:
Units on planning and time management

How to:
1. Review Lesson VI and discuss any questions about the lesson.
2. Discuss steps and techniques used in planning.
3. Discuss what makes a good plan.
4. Develop the elements in the QC plan outline into suitable verbiage for inclusion in QC/QA department five-year plan.
5. Discuss the results of the planning exercise.
6. Discuss management by objectives.
7. Discuss time management and develop a time-management matrix to determine daily time usage.

Conclusions:
1. Developed a matrix for time usage.
2. Students expounded on QC plan outline elements.

Assignment:
Read the units on organizing and organizations, pages 87-108.

Comments:

Lesson VIII. Organizing and the Organization

Goal:
1. To recognize organizing as a supervisory skill.
2. To examine the structure and make-up of organizations.
3. To be able to conduct an interview and performance appraisals.

Materials:
Unit on organizing and organizations

How to:
1. Review Lesson VII and discuss any questions from the unit.
2. Talk about organizing and ways to organize.
3. Discuss organizational structure and hazards.
4. Have the students draw an organization chart for their respective companies.
5. Discuss with the group staffing and the process of interviewing.
6. Conduct an interview by role playing, page 97.
7. Discuss performance reviews (appraisals) and complete exercise on performance reviews, page 100.
8. Role play conducting performance reviews, page 102.

Conclusions:
    1. Developed organization chart for company.
    2. Wrote job description.
    3. Role played interviewing and performance reviewing.

Assignment:
    Read units on delegation and budgeting, pages 109-120.

Comments:

Lesson IX. Delegation and Budgeting

Goal:
    To determine the best ways to delegate and budget.

Materials:
    Units on delegation and budgets

How to:
    1. Review Lesson VIII and answer any questions about that unit.
    2. Discuss the degrees of delegation and how to delegate.
    3. Complete and discuss the case study: "Do You Delegate?" on page 112.
    4. Discuss budgets as a control device.
    5. Discuss the sample budget.
    6. Have each student work up a home budget.
    7. Discuss the benefits of budgets.

Conclusions:
    1. Students gained knowledge of delegation and budgets.
    2. Practiced tracking income and expenses.

Assignment:
    1. Read the unit on labor relations, pages 121-124.
    2. Ask students to determine what they have gained from this course and the separate topics.

Comments:

Lesson X. Labor Relations

Goal:
To provide information on labor relations.

Materials:
Unit on labor relations
Film

How to:
1. Review Lesson IX and answer any questions about the lesson.
2. Discuss the role of labor relations in the union and nonunion organizations.
3. Discuss grievance and arbitration procedures.
4. Students retake the self-examination exercise on page 127.
5. Summary of the course is given. Determine with a questionnaire if the students completed their goals and objectives.
6. Issue grades and hand out certificates.
7. Thank everyone for attending the class.

Conclusions:
1. Discussed labor relations.
2. Students completed questionnaire.

Assignment:
Suggest to the group that the self-examination exercise should be completed again in six months to see "where you are."

Comments:

WORK FORCE

"WHO IS THE WORK FORCE?"

The information we will be exchanging throughout this course may be a review for some of you, but we need to have a starting place. Our starting place will be to develop a philosophy about our relationship with our supervisor, manager, peers, subordinates, and to determine who we are as individuals. This philosophy includes the job we do, or hope to experience. In general terms, we start with the work force.

All of us are part of the work force. We come from all walks of life. Some of us are young, old, men, women, black, native American, Chicano, Asian, etc. We have needs, desires, dreams, and expectations. However, these needs may not be fulfilled because of discrimination, on the basis of society, culture, age, sex, race, creed, or sexual preference. Some individuals or groups have stated openly that these differences are enough not to allow any so-called "different" individual to have a job or a place in American society. These biases, stereotypes, and discriminatory attitudes are, unfortunately, part of all of our lives.

To help equalize the work force and allow for fairness in labor practices, the Federal Government has enacted a series of laws. Two such laws are:

1. *Equal Pay Amendment (1963) of the Fair Labor Standards Act of 1938.*
   This act was designed to end discrimination, but from the standpoint of pay, the act has not been effective.
2. *Title VII of the Civil Rights Acts of 1964.*
   This act was designed to neutralize any kind of discrimination in employment practices against women. The courts have not seen this act in the way it was intended. The act has not been effective.

In 1975, the Department of Labor conducted a salary survey comparing the wages of men and women. The study showed that:

1. Male wage earners brought home a median income of $12,770, compared to $7,531 by females doing the same job with the same education.
2. Men with a college education had a median income of $17,861, compared with $10,861 for females with the same education and job.

By 1984, the problem of comparable wages had not decreased, but in fact had increased. The increase in the differences in wages had grown at a faster rate than in the time period of the first study. In 1986, women, on the average, are being paid 30% less than men. Wage differences do not just apply to women in the work force, but to all minority groups and individuals.

Managing The Work Force

As a supervisor or manager, we need to examine the biases, stereotypes, and discriminatory attitudes we have toward all individuals in the work force. We may find out we have made some errors in our judgment of people. When examining the different reasons why people work, we come face to face with very old biases.

Over the years, we have heard that women work because they just want some "pin money." Most of us would agree that the real reason women work is the same reason all of us work — *economics*. The number of women working outside the home has increased over the years. In 1900, one out of every twenty married women worked outside of the home, and two out of every three single women worked outside of the home.[1] By 1981, over 60% of all women were working outside their homes.[1]

Another area where perhaps biases and stereotypes have clouded our views as supervisors and managers is absenteeism. A Department of Labor study conducted in the last decade examined the differences between groups of men and women as to their turnover and absenteeism rates. The study concluded that women were not absent any more as a group than any other group. Further, in individual groups, women were more reliable than men.

As supervisors and managers, we need to look at the *real* causes of problems created by individuals, *not* at the archaic prejudices and stereotypes of any minority group these individuals may represent.

One possible cause of absenteeism may be the job. The job may be just plain boring. The RCA Corporation conducted a study using 112 women employees who had a very high rate of tardiness and absenteeism at their desk jobs. These women were switched to material handling positions that were exclusively held by men. The material handling jobs included: lifting 50 pound cartons, shifting 55 gallon drums, and lift-truck driving. The results of this study were:

1. The women liked the material handling positions.
2. Safety and housekeeping in the stock areas were vastly improved.
3. Their record of tardiness and absenteeism was near perfect.[2]

Some companies have made a decision to equalize the work force by writing and enforcing sexual harassment policies. Here is an example of a typical sexual harassment policy for your discussion.

LEADER:
Have students read over Sexual Harassment Policy. Initiate discussion, drawing from your own and students' experiences or information.

SEXUAL HARASSMENT POLICY

Purpose

To establish a company policy regarding sexual harassment in the work place.

Definition

Sexual harassment as defined by the EQUAL EMPLOYMENT OPPORTUNITY COMMISSION:
Unwelcome sexual advances, requests for sexual favors, and other verbal or physical contact of a sexual nature constitute sexual harassment when:

1. Submission is made explicitly a condition of employment.
2. Submission or rejection is used as the basis for employment decisions.
3. Such conduct interferes with an individual's work performance or creates an intimidating, hostile, or offensive working environment.

Statement of Policy

It is the policy of this company that any form of sexual harassment is unacceptable behavior and is subject to disciplinary action up to and including termination.

Any employee who has witnessed or been the recipient of sexual harassment is encouraged to contact their supervisor or the Personnel Manager. An investigation of the allegations will be conducted, respecting the rights of all parties involved. If facts support the allegation, appropriate disciplinary action will be taken up to and including termination.

This policy applies equally to both sexes and all levels of employees.

Another area of bias and stereotypes is the difference between black and white employees in the work force. The Foremanship Foundation conducted a survey in 1970 that addressed the racial relationships between black employees and white employees. The study concluded with the following results:

1. Of the individuals surveyed, 58% felt that black and white employee performances are the same.
2. Of the individuals surveyed, 2% stated that they felt black employees do a better job than white employees.
3. Of the individuals surveyed, 40% answered that they felt white employees are better than black employees.[3]

Supervisors and managers in the surveyed group were older and with long tenure. They indicated a prejudice against blacks, women, and other minority groups. The less educated felt their jobs were threatened by black and other minority groups.

The next two groups of people within the total work force are divided by age. The first group consists of individuals under 25 years of age, and the second group includes individuals who would be considered "older" workers.

The issues for the 25 years of age or younger group are:
1. They generally want the same rights as their manager or supervisor.
2. They do not want to work where their health or safety is endangered.
3. They expect improvements to be made fast.[4]

Compare these issues of the 25 years of age or younger workers with the "older" workers. This group has special needs and requirements, but they want to be treated fairly, honestly, and consistently.

We, as supervisors and managers, need to address a fact of life that all of us will experience the worries, concerns, and fears of getting older. We can relate to aging because of our own aging process, but we may not want to accept it.

Consider that the physical aging process occurs as early as age ten — especially with some functions of the ears and eyes. There is a 60% reduction in an individual's peak physical ability by 60 years of age. Of course, this reduction of physical ability differs from one individual to another.

This older age group does have a number of attributes that some individuals overlook. Workers 60 years of age or over are as good as — if not superior — to the average younger workers in absenteeism, dependability, work quality, work volume, judgment, and human relations.

Special considerations for older workers, but which may also apply to all workers, are the problems that occur during the aging process. These problems include reduced hearing, reduced memory, and reduced vision.

A supervisor or manager can counteract the possibility of these problems occurring by:
1. Giving clear information and directions.
2. Training and providing work aids.
3. Providing for better illumination and contrast in colors. (Remember, when you place red and blue colors together, the eyes cannot distinguish the line between these two colors. The dividing line will appear to be curved, rough, and generally undistinguishable.)

How do you deal, as a supervisor or manager, with these different groups of people in the work force? Some suggestions include:
1. Treat your employees as individuals instead of a group.
2. Use your authority only within reason.
3. Seek to improve the working conditions in the work place.
4. Learn to be flexible.
5. Convey the meaning of each assignment.
6. Enrich the nature of the work and job.
7. See that each individual has a meaningful job.
8. Modify the job to match the interests of the individual as best as possible.
9. Talk with your employees, and *listen* to what they are saying.

The work force is also us; that is, you and me. Do you have any other suggestions?

LEADER:
Write each suggestion on the chalkboard or other visual aid, and reinforce each individual's ideas.

"What Makes a Supervisor or Manager?"

As beginning or seasoned professional supervisors and managers, we need to have a common ground to build and process on the job. Let's start with some basic questions and discussion topics.

The first question to answer is: *"What makes a supervisor?"* This question may seem easy to answer on the surface, but let us examine it in detail. Here is a list of what a supervisor can be. What other qualities can you suggest to add to this list?

A supervisor:
1. Leads.
2. Plans effectively.

3. Provides technical information and expertise.
4. Mediates between management and other employees.
5. Provides a climate of positive human relations.
6. Shapes positive employee attitudes.
7. Interprets and applies the organization's policies, work orders and jobs.
8. Trains and instructs employees to work efficiently and effectively.
9. Counsels and disciplines employees, and provides other personnel functions.
10. Plans and maintains employee work schedules.
11. Coordinates department work procedures effectively and efficiently.
12. Takes the necessary steps to secure a *quality* product or service.

LEADER:
Ask the students to come up with their own ideas. Write them down on the chalkboard or other visual aid so all of the students can see the list. Discuss each idea, having the group draw from their own experiences and observations.

The second question is *"What makes a manager?"* A manager performs five basic functions or tasks:
1. PLANNING: Determines what to do in advance.
2. ORGANIZING: Divides work and tasks to be completed.
3. STAFFING: Recruits new employees and determines what qualified individuals can complete the required tasks.
4. DIRECTING: Guides, stimulates, and supervises employees in completing required tasks.
5. CONTROLS: Takes the necessary steps to achieve the department and company goals and objectives: e.g., budgets.

Now, you have some idea in general terms what a supervisor and manager do for their wages. The next question to address is *"What is a good supervisor or manager?"* What are some of your thoughts?

Good supervisory or management qualities may include:
1. Making sure the workers are able to do the job they are being paid to complete.
2. Making sure each individual knows what they are expected to contribute and expected to complete.
3. Staffing the department with individual strengths in mind.
4. Being honest, fair, and consistent.
5. Motivating employees to excel at their jobs.

Here is an exercise for you to complete. This exercise is to list the ten characteristics, one being the most important and ten being the least important, that best describe the ideal supervisor. This list can be used by each student as a goal for being a good supervisor or manager.

THE IDEAL SUPERVISOR OR MANAGER EXERCISE

Directions:

Using the words below, number the 13 words that BEST DESCRIBE the ideal supervisor or manager to you. Number one being the word that best describes your concept of the ideal supervisor or manager, and number 13 would be the word that least describes your concept of the ideal supervisor or manager.

A discussion of this exercise will follow the completion of your selections.

_____ Aggressive	_____ Kind	_____ Dependable
_____ Innovative	_____ Self-Confident	_____ Calculating
_____ Knowledgeable	_____ Logical	_____ Powerful
_____ Honest	_____ Critical	_____ Firm
_____ Competent	_____ Humorous	_____ Fair

_____ Just   _____ Patient   _____ Independent
_____ Thorough   _____ Calm   _____ Friendly

LEADER:

After all the students have completed the exercise, write the characteristics on the chalkboard or other visual aid so all of the students can read them. This will show you what the students think and feel are important to them, and it will give the students some idea that they are not alone with their ideas and thoughts.

Results from Past Classes on Ideal Supervisor/Manager Exercise

LEADER:

After your discussion of what the students consider to be the most important characteristics for the ideal supervisor or manager, compare the results of past classes with the present results.

The following results reflect the opinions of classes conducted 1978 through 1986:

Characteristic	**Number of Times Indicated as Number 1**
Dependable	126
Knowledgeable	123
Self-Confident	114
Honest	113
Fair	102
Competent	87
Patient	84
Thorough	75
Friendly	60
Innovative	54
Firm	53
Logical	49
Calm	41

Basing this information on what students have considered as the ideal supervisor or manager, one conclusion is: *People want dependable, knowledgeable, self-confident, honest, and fair supervisors and managers. They want to become like those supervisors.*

LEADER:

The reasons for these choices can be used as further discussion points in advanced groups. One question to use as a lead-in for discussion may be: "Why do you feel people have picked a supervisor or manager with these characteristics?"

We started with the general work force as a group, and then divided the total work force into subgroups. The subgroups were then divided into even smaller groups, and finally we reach one person in the work force — that person is you. We need to know about ourselves as individuals. We need to know what makes us tick emotionally and physically before we handle other people. We may not come to "know" everything about ourselves, but we may become better aware of not only our limitations, but also our capabilities.

Who are you? What do you do? Are you a leader? Can you handle the stress? Can you communicate to others? Questions go on and on for each of us; we need some direction, and this is what this material and course can do.

To help you determine the answers to most of these personal questions, here is an exercise to help you. This exercise is to provide a way for you to analyze by thoughtfully and honestly answering the questions in the exercise. The results are for your use and would be considered confidential, so be direct and honest with yourself.

Complete the exercise.

SELF-EXAMINATION EXERCISE

You are to analyze yourself by thoughtfully and honestly answering the ten category questions. In answering each question in each category, grade yourself by using the following scale:

4 . . . . . . Superior
3 . . . . . . Above Average
2 . . . . . . Average
1 . . . . . . Below Average

Once you have graded each question, place your total in the space provided in the "Your Present Strengths Summary" at the end of this exercise.

The results are for your confidential use, so please be direct and honest with yourself.

1. Aspiration
   _____ A. Can you describe your life goal in logical terms?
   _____ B. Does your goal challenge the very utmost of your ability?
   _____ C. Have you worked out a plan for attaining your goal?
   _____ D. Are you ready to give up other aims and pleasures to be successful?

2. Knowledge
   _____ A. How does your present knowledge compare with knowledge that is possible to gain?
   _____ B. Do you faithfully follow the rule of gaining knowledge when needed?
   _____ C. How much pride do you take in learning something new daily?
   _____ D. To what extent are you open to new knowledge, ideas, and methods?

3. Ambition
   _____ A. When you see something that should be done, do you consistently start right out to do it?
   _____ B. Are you willing to work before or after hours to develop new ideas connected with your job?
   _____ C. Are you willing to share your ideas with others?
   _____ D. Is your initiative backed up by determination to finish what you start?

4. Thoroughness
   _____ A. Do your efforts go beyond what you have been asked to do?
   _____ B. Do you perform disagreeable tasks?
   _____ C. When you have something to do, do you search for the very best way of accomplishing it?
   _____ D. Do you refuse to pass judgment on any matter until all the facts have been weighed?

5. Investigative Powers
   _____ A. Do you frequently see ways of making practical use of information that comes to you daily?
   _____ B. Do you think something through to form your own opinions rather than accepting the opinions of others?
   _____ C. Do you "dig down" to get at the bottom of problems?
   _____ D. When you have all the facts, how successful are you in rejecting personal prejudice and other people's biased opinions?

6. Decision Making
   _____ A. How much satisfaction do you find in your responsibility for important decisions?

_____ B. To what extent are your decisions based on well thought-out reasons?
_____ C. Do you procrastinate in making final decisions on important questions?
_____ D. When you have made a decision, how confidently do you put it into effect?

7. Leadership

_____ A. How much confidence do you have when you know you are right?
_____ B. Are you considerate of the rights and feelings of others?
_____ C. Do you retain the good will of your associates when you have to criticize them?
_____ D. Do you believe your associates listen to your views or concepts with confidence and respect?
_____ E. Do you inspire confidence in others?
_____ F. Do you meet criticism without losing your temper?

8. Organizing Ability

_____ A. Do you analyze the problems that confront you?
_____ B. Are you successful in separating tasks into smaller ones your employees can more easily complete?
_____ C. Do you follow a systematic plan in assigning and doing tasks?

9. Problem Solving

_____ A. Do you develop new ideas to use in solving problems?
_____ B. When things are going wrong do you suggest ways for improving them?
_____ C. Do you study what you do with the intent of finding a better way to complete it?
_____ D. Do your employees and peers consider your ideas practical?

10. Application

_____ A. Do you analyze your successes or failures?
_____ B. Do you analyze the success or failure of others?
_____ C. Are you the first person to suggest a practical solution to a problem?
_____ D. Do you learn the principles that apply to work other than your own for a total view?

Your Present Strengths Summary

_____ 1. Aspiration
_____ 2. Knowledge
_____ 3. Ambition
_____ 4. Thoroughness
_____ 5. Investigative Powers
_____ 6. Decision Making
_____ 7. Leadership
_____ 8. Organizing Ability
_____ 9. Problem Solving
_____ 10. Application

Keep this summary for your records, and review this exercise six months from the date you first completed the exercise.

This exercise is designed to give the individual a starting point to build and grow as a supervisor and manager. It is also designed to provide the individual an inventory of personal areas where work can be completed, and of personal areas that show individual strengths and weaknesses. Other uses for this exercise would be in developing a career plan, as a confidence builder for the students, and in demonstrating the possibility of growth patterns for your employees.

HELP . . . STRESS!

As individuals, in order to live happy lives, we need to learn how to deal with the stresses of American society. Stress can destroy each of us; it is important to recognize its effects on us and for us to learn how to deal with it. This understanding of stress helps us acknowledge the fact that we are *all* under pressure in one way or another.

The type of work we do is stressful. The type of lifestyles we lead are stressful. Dealing with jobs, families, and other daily activities is stressful. Yet, for some individuals, stress is at a manageable level. However, experiencing too much stress can result in heart attacks, canker sores, drug abuse (over-the-counter as well as under-the-counter), ulcers, etc. But stress itself is not the sole cause of these problems.

This material is not designed to deeply analyze stress and its resulting complications, but it is designed for you to take a closer look at yourself and determine if changes are needed for you. It is only then that you can deal with *others* in an honest, fair, and caring manner. Be aware of your body signals; your body may be telling you something.

Some of the ways of managing your stress are to:

1. Eat balanced meals and get plenty of sleep.
2. Watch your weight.
3. Watch your smoking and drinking habits.
4. Learn relaxation techniques.
5. Have one or more friends to confide in about personal matters.
6. Speak openly about your feelings when you are angry or worried.
7. Do something for fun at least once a week!

These statements can be aids for you in dealing with stress. However, these are just suggestions. If you want and need further help, see your doctor. You may even use other aids that work for you.

After you have reached inside of yourself and made a determination of who you are, the next step is to explore your skill development. The skills of *leadership, communications, organization, planning, staffing,* and *controlling*. These skills need to be developed and refined.

FOOTNOTES

1. Bittel, Lester R. *What Every Supervisor Should Know.* New York, N.Y.: McGraw-Hill, 1974, p. 316.
2. Ibid, p. 324.
3. Ibid, p. 385.
4. Ibid, pp. 381-82.

LEADERSHIP

LEADERSHIP

Leadership is the first skill considered for development in this material. We'll start the leadership development with an exercise.

LEADER:

   The students, in doing this exercise, would follow these simple instructions: The students are to circle the best answer to each question. (They may not be able to come up with one answer, but allow them to work to try to get one answer.) Divide the students into small groups once they have completed the exercise. Give the students the following instructions:
   1. Divide into small groups of three, five, seven, etc. This makes it easier to make decisions in the groups.
   2. In your groups, follow these six points:
      a. Pick a leader, and think about how you picked that person.
      b. Discuss the answers you have given in the exercise.
      c. Come up with one set of answers for the group. Think about and write down how your group completed this task.
      d. Your groups will need to make the decisions and rules for this exercise.
      e. During this exercise try to defend your answers, but the goal is to have only one set of answers at the end of the 30 minutes allowed for this exercise.
      f. After the exercise discussions, be prepared to discuss your answers; discuss the selection of a leader, how the process went, and your general comments.
   3. Direct the students to the different locations for the group activity.
   4. The students can pick their groups, all the instructor needs to do is show the students where the groups can meet and how many people are in each group.
   5. Final instructions to the group of students are: watch, listen, question, and draw your conclusions from the activities in each group.

LEADERSHIP EXERCISE

Directions: Circle the *best* answer for each question.

1. Your employees have not been responding to your obvious concern for their welfare, and their performance has taken a nose dive.
    A. Emphasize the use of procedures and processes for task accomplishments.
    B. Make yourself available for discussion but do not force yourself on the group.
    C. Talk with the employees and set up goals and objectives to be completed.
    D. Be careful not to intervene.

2. You have observed the performance of your group has improved. You have been making sure that all members are aware of their roles and objectives.
    A. Engage in friendly conversation, but continue to make sure that all members are aware of their roles and objectives.
    B. Take no definite action.
    C. Do what you can to make the group feel important and involved.
    D. Emphasize the importance of deadlines and tasks to be completed.

3. Members of your group are unable to solve a problem themselves. You have normally left them alone and their performance and personal working relations have been good.
    A. Involve the group and together engage in problem-solving techniques.
    B. Let the group work it out.
    C. Act quickly and firmly to correct and redirect the group.
    D. Encourage the group to work on the problem and be available for any help or discussion.

4. You are considering a major change. Your employees have an excellent record of accomplishment. They respect you as their leader and the need for change.
   A. Allow for group involvement in making the change, but do not force them.
   B. Announce the changes and then implement them with close supervision.
   C. Allow the group to develop its own direction.
   D. Incorporate group recommendations, but you direct the change.

5. The performance of your group has been dropping during the last few months and the members of the group have been unconcerned with meeting goals and objectives. In the past, redefining the goals and objectives helped, but it did not last.
   A. Allow the group to develop its own direction.
   B. Incorporate group recommendations, but see that the objectives are completed on time.
   C. Redefine the goals and objectives and supervise carefully.
   D. Allow the group to be involved in the setting of the goals and objectives, but do not force them.

6. You have stepped into an efficiently run situation. The previous supervisor was good, and you want to maintain the productive environment but you would like to begin to humanize the department.
   A. Do what you can to make the group feel important and involved.
   B. Emphasize the importance of deadlines, timetables, and tasks.
   C. Be careful not to intervene.
   D. Get the group involved in decision-making tasks, but see that the goals and objectives are achieved and maintained.

7. You are considering major changes in your department structure. You have asked and received suggestions from your employees about the changes needed. The group has demonstrated flexibility in the daily operations of the department.
   A. Define the change and supervise carefully.
   B. Allow the members of the group to organize and complete the changes in the department.
   C. Make the needed changes and maintain control of the situation.
   D. Avoid confrontation and do not apply pressure.

8. Your superior has appointed you to head a task force to recommend changes. The group is not clear about its goals. Attendance at the sessions has been poor, and the meetings have turned into social gatherings. The group has the potential and talent to complete the work required.
   A. Let the group work it out.
   B. Incorporate the group recommendations, but see that the goals and objectives are completed.
   C. Define the goals and objectives and supervise carefully.
   D. Allow the group to be involved in setting goals and objectives, but do not force your opinions on the group.

9. Recent information indicates some internal difficulties among your employees. The group works well together and they have a remarkable record of completing tasks in an effective manner.
   A. Try out your solutions with the employees and examine the need for changes.
   B. Allow the group to work out the problem.
   C. Act quickly and firmly to correct and direct the group.
   D. Make yourself available for discussion.

10. Your employees are able to take responsibility, but are not responding to your recent definition of procedures and standards.
    A. Allow the group to be involved in defining procedures and standards, but do not force your opinions on the group.
    B. Define the procedures and standards and supervise carefully.
    C. Avoid confrontation.
    D. Incorporate the group recommendations and see that the new procedures and standards are completed.

11. You have been promoted to a new position. The previous supervisor was uninvolved in the affairs of

the group. The group handled its tasks and directions very well and interacted positively.
A. Take steps to lead employees toward working in a well-directed manner.
B. Involve employees in decision making and reinforce good results.
C. Discuss past performance with the group and examine the need for different goals and objectives.
D. Do nothing.

Exercise Review
LEADER:
  1. *After 30 minutes of group activity, ask each group the following questions:*
     a. *"How did you select your group leader?" (All answers are acceptable.)*
     b. *"How did you get the answers you got during your discussion period?"*
     c. *"Go ahead and explain the process, method, and techniques you used to come up with one set of answers."*

     This exercise is designed to provide individuals with information about their style of leadership. It is not important to place a name on the different styles of leadership. It is an individual style that is now acknowledged by each person. Once each person has an idea of what his style of leadership is, he can make changes or strengthen his style.
  2. *Another part of this exercise was to simulate a business meeting. The individuals completed a task in a short period of time, with varied disciplines found in a business climate.*

Team or Participative Leadership Style

There are different leadership styles that could be considered, but for the purpose of this material the only style of leadership that will be discussed is *team* or *participative*. This style of leadership allows for participation of the employees in making decisions. By sharing in the decision-making process, the employees become more committed to the decision and its results.

The team or participative management leadership style brings a wide range of expertise to the process of making decisions by drawing on all employees for their input. Not all employees want to share in this process, however. With a team-style approach to leadership, the decision-making process will take longer to achieve, but the result will have a longer effect on the individuals, department, and organization.

Basically, the group makes the decision, and the team leader controls and stimulates the group for total effectiveness.

What style of leadership is best for *me*?

The most effective leadership style for you is one that is compatible with your personality, value system, work force, and environment. Take time to understand yourself and the needs of your employees. People have a whole range of wants and needs that require fulfilling. Remember, some individuals prefer job security with little or no responsibilities; other individuals seek more job satisfaction — especially through decision-making participation.

Your leadership style should come from a conscious analysis of yourself and your employees.

"How Many of You Are Leaders?"

Think in terms that all of you are leaders. You have taken the risk to read this material and you are taking this course. Now, you may not be a leader in all aspects of your life, but you, like other people, show leadership abilities and skills that you may not acknowledge.

"What is *your* definition of a leader?"

LEADER:
  Write the answers on the chalkboard or some other visual aid so all the students can see the comments.

Leadership Skills

A leader:

1. Has goals in mind.
2. Makes choices of personal behavior.
3. Influences the behavior of others. The style of influence will determine how a group accepts or rejects the leader.
4. Is persuasive.
5. Has a pattern of leadership. The pattern of leadership allows for:
    a. Freedom of expression in your group by all members (common within Quality Circles).
    b. Guiding the group, but not providing solutions. The group must provide the solutions and function on its own.
    c. Accepting all thoughts from all group members. No person's ideas are to be put down. Each person has the freedom to express thoughts within the group.
    d. Bringing out ideas from *all* individuals in the group. If one person is controlling the discussion, the leader needs to direct the group in the direction of the group's objectives. As leader, one approach would be to say, "We have heard from (the person's name), but we have not heard from (the person's name)." This will direct the discussion to others and give the opportunity for more ideas to flow from the group.
    e. Being supportive. Let the group know that their ideas, concepts, recommendations, results, etc., are acceptable.
    f. Waiting out pauses. Allow the group to fill in the pauses that may occur during a discussion period. Practice waiting out these pauses. Normally, the silence would be filled by someone, but it should not be the leader.
    g. Protecting the minority view. Remember each person has an equal opportunity to have his view expressed. If possible, use a personal example on the importance of this concept — especially in the quality area.
    h. Restating the problem if the discussion gets off track.
    i. Separating solutions and evaluations during the group discussions.
    j. Allowing for different evaluations of problems.
    k. Adapting to the situation and being a flexible leader.
    l. Not jeopardizing your personal integrity, nor allowing unethical behavior toward others in any situation.
    m. Summarizing the group's progress or decisions.

Use Your Leadership Skills in Meetings

Your leadership skills can be practiced in many different ways with very good results. You can practice in business situations, as well as in your home life. Using the department meeting as your first practice session in a business situation; you can follow the pattern of leadership and leadership style discussed earlier. Remember, you have the power to control what happens in the meeting.

All of us have been in meetings that just did not work, for one or more different reasons. A poor meeting may have one or more characteristics that cause you frustration.

Have you ever been in a meeting where:

There were too many participants. The meetings lasted for hours or at least seemed to last forever. The meetings were held too frequent or out of habit. The wrong people were included in the meeting. There were no visual nor written aids to illustrate a point or concept. No pre-notice, purpose, nor agenda for the meeting was available before the group met. There was no real reason to be there. The meeting place was dirty, noisy, or poorly lit. Interruptions by the telephone and people occurred during the meeting. No organization or plan for the meeting was known by either the leader or the members of the group. No real starting or ending time for the meeting was given. There was more than one meeting occurring at the same time (chitchat, arguments, hostilities of sorts, war stories, etc.). Too much control by the leader or by other members in the meeting. The meeting was premature, and poor participation was common for many meetings.

You may be able to come up with other causes for poor meetings. Let's correct the problems. You can do it. Both the leader and attendees have a responsibility for making meetings run smoothly and effectively. However, first the leader must:
1. Provide an agenda for the meeting and establish a time limit for each topic. (See example below.)
2. Develop a plan.
3. Determine who should be included in the meeting and how many individuals should participate.
4. Determine a time, place, date, topic, tools, equipment, etc., needed to make for an effective meeting.
5. Write a memo to the personnel to be included in the meeting specifying the meeting place, time, and date.
6. During the meeting, practice the pattern of leadership skills discussed earlier.

Sample Agenda for Quality Control Meeting

I. Problems of the Week.
   A. Discuss with group.
   B. Explore possible solutions.
II. Personnel's Personal Objectives.
   A. How are individuals doing with their objectives?
   B. What objectives have been completed?
   C. Any further discussion?
III. New Projects.
   A. List the new projects available.
   B. Who wants to work on one or more projects?
   C. Discuss methods and techniques.
   D. Decide due dates.
IV. Training Topic.
   A. What is the training topic?
   B. Introduce person doing training topic.
   C. Review the last training topic.
   D. Who wants to do the next training topic? (Or assign.)
   E. Follow-up.
V. Provide company and department information.
VI. Questions.

Control the Meeting — It is up to YOU

As the leader, you are in control of the situation. This applies to the meeting. Use the discussed pattern of leadership skills to your advantage in conducting an effective meeting.

Remember, you do not have to resolve the problems in one meeting. You may choose to break the group into smaller teams to investigate the entire problem or only a small part of it. The smaller group would then report their findings to the whole group at a later date, time, and place. If this meeting is a brainstorming session, limit your time to approximately 25 minutes. This rule of thumb allows for fresh ideas and concepts as well as the effective use of every individual's time. When brainstorming sessions extend for longer periods of time, the group members usually experience mental fatigue. The same ideas seem to get repeated, only in different words.

The *time* of day as well as the *day* of meetings are important. In order to control the meetings, you may want to have them in the late morning. Try to hold the meetings before noon because most people do not want to miss their lunch break. They will be more willing to end the meetings on time. Normally, people are more active in the morning hours than in the afternoon. This is especially true in societies and cultures where heavy midday meals are consumed. With heavy lunches, bodies spend a lot of time digesting the food, but not much time is spent thinking.

The day of the week is important — especially when weekends, vacations, holidays, and days off fall before or right after the scheduled meeting. People's creative energy may be channeled to these outside activities rather than the meeting itself.

The leader has a number of responsibilities to see that the meetings are effectively directed. The members also have responsibilities.

As a member in a meeting, what can you do to see that the meeting is effective?

LEADER:
Discuss and write the ideas on the chalkboard, and now is a good time to reinforce the patterns of leadership skills.

Meetings Are for the Participation of All

Points highlighting member participation should include:

1. Trusting the other group members and leader.
2. Sharing information openly and honestly.
3. Dealing in facts and keeping emotions at a minimum.
4. Seeing disagreements as opportunities, not personal attacks.
5. Asking questions.
6. Being objective.
7. Waiting for solutions until all the facts are presented.
8. Viewing the leader as a guide to help direct the group.

CASE STUDY: PRACTICING LEADERSHIP SKILLS

Since practicing skills, especially new ones, can be frustrating at best, analyze and review the following case study.

Directions:

1. Read the case study carefully and answer the questions. After you have completed the case, you will break into small groups. In the small groups, pick a leader. (Try not to pick a leader who was a leader in the last exercise.) Come up with *one* set of answers based on your group discussion.
2. As the leader, remember to follow the pattern of leadership skills and the responsibilities you have to the group and yourself.
3. As a group member, follow the responsibilities you have to see that the group is effective.
4. You have a 30 minute time limit. Once your time is up, be prepared to discuss your ideas and how you used your leadership and group member skills.

"Who's Running My Department?"

I am supervisor of the Quality Control Laboratory in my organization. I am having trouble with one of my technicians. The technician has been in the department for over two years. Every time I give my employees instructions, they first go and check with my "problem" technician to determine if they should follow them and end up following my instructions, anyway.

I really resent the fact that the group simply will not follow my directions. The technician is a good worker. Although I have been looking for reasons to get rid of him, I have not found anything that would stand up.

It seems to me that the technician exercises power over the group and that he has the group exactly where he wants them. Recently, the "problem" technician has been fine, but I have a feeling the problem will occur again. It is only a matter of time.

What do I do?

Questions to answer:

1. What are the major problems in this case?

2. What would your suggestions be?
3. What are the choices that could be made?
4. What are the advantages and disadvantages of each choice?
5. How can this type of problem be corrected before it develops into a situation that cannot be resolved?
6. How would you deal with this situation if you were the manager of the person discussing the problem?
7. Could you involve the personnel manager in this case, and what might be his/her reaction?

SUMMARY

Effective meetings should have three very important ingredients. These ingredients are: the *leader*, the *members*, and the *meeting* itself.

Ingredient one is the *leader*.

The leader needs to:

1. Accept information without first evaluating it.
2. Make the information visible.
3. Encourage members to respond to one another.
4. Avoid forcing personal opinions and solutions.
5. Summarize periodically to indicate the meeting's progress and direction.
6. State the situation or problem in objective terms.
7. Share relevant information to all group members.
8. Ask questions.
9. Not judge one idea or concept better than another because of personal bias.

The second ingredient for an effective meeting is each *member*.

Each member needs to:

1. Trust in other group members.
2. Share information relevant to the group and meeting.
3. Show a minimum amount of emotion.
4. Discuss items from a factual standpoint.
5. Not view disagreement as a threat.
6. Ask questions.
7. Have an objective attitude.
8. See the group leader as a guide.
9. Wait until the discussion is completed before offering personal comments.

The third and last ingredient for an effective meeting is the *meeting* itself.

The meeting needs to:

1. Have an agenda.
2. Start on time.
3. Have a reason or objective for the meeting.
4. Have a goal and objective.
5. Have a location and time set for starting and ending.
6. Have an open environment where discussion can occur without bias.
7. Have individuals who can contribute to the discussion.

COMMUNICATION

COMMUNICATION

This chapter deals with different types of communication, communication skills, and the effect of good and bad communication on the sender and receiver.

Communication includes:
- A. Talking to each other.
- B. Talking and listening to each other.
- C. Writing to one another.
- D. Actively listening.

LEADER:

Write on the chalkboard ideas generated by the students to the question "What is communication?".

ONE- AND TWO-WAY COMMUNICATION EXERCISES

Sometimes we view communication in terms of either one- or two-way communication. As supervisors and managers, there needs to be effective communication from effective communicators. Your instructor will present two exercises that will enable you to practice establishing good effective verbal communication skills in one-way and two-way communication arrangements.

LEADER

1. *Ask for a volunteer from the students. Do not pick a student. Give the volunteer a copy of the one-way communication design below. Have the volunteer describe the design to the group. Instruct the group that they cannot ask any questions. This is an example of one-way communication. Once the volunteer has completed the exercise, have him show the group what the actual design looks like.*

2. Next have the same volunteer describe the two-way communication design. However, this time the group can ask questions of the volunteer. This is an example of two-way communication. After the volunteer has completed describing the design, have him show this design to the group, also.

3. Discuss with the volunteer and the group how each felt during the one- and two-way communication exercises.

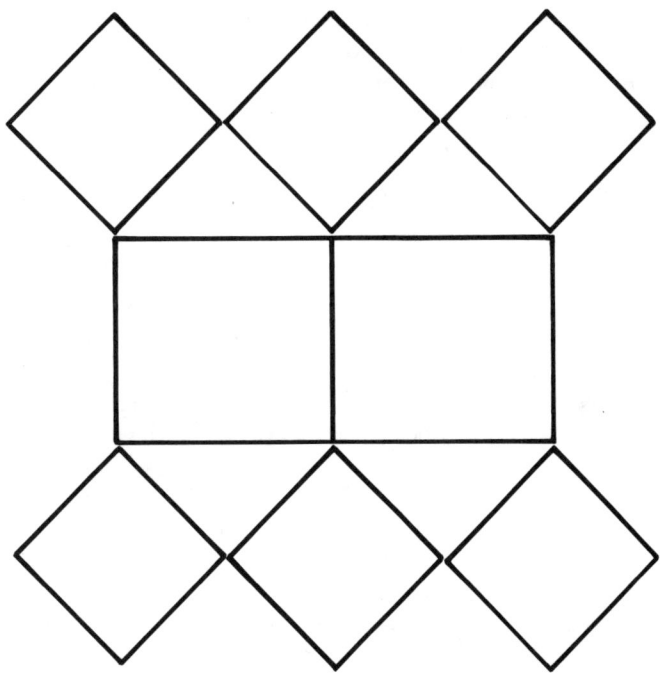

Example of One-Way Communication

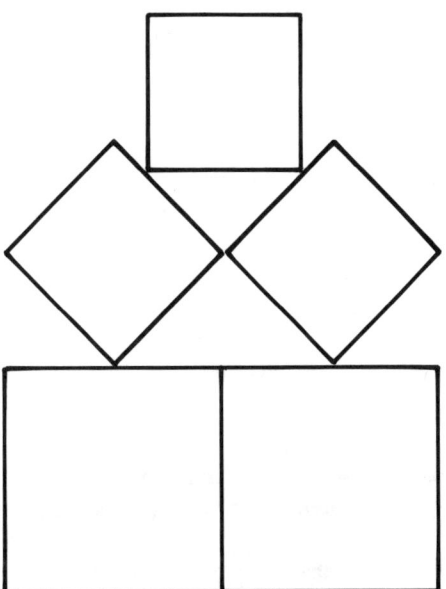

Example of Two-Way Communication

Normally, the two-way communication exercise is much easier to deal with for the volunteer and the group. However, two-way communication does not always work in the work place. Do not be concerned about the conclusions in the classroom. The purpose of these exercises is to demonstrate the differences and problems with one- and two-way communication.

PERSONAL TWO-WAY COMMUNICATION EXERCISE

Another exercise involves a more personal two-way communication experience. The general instructions are that everyone divides into groups of two people. If there is an uneven number of individuals in the total group, the leader can become part of the exercise. Note: The objectives for this exercise are for you to:

1. Use two-way communication skills.
2. Use listening as part of the communication process.
3. Use more than verbal communication skills — use listening and writing skills, also.
4. Acquire better knowledge of each other and experience a group bonding.

LEADER:
1. *Ask the students to divide into groups of two persons.*
2. *Each person will have five minutes to find out about the other person. During these five minutes, you can take notes and ask questions.*
3. *Change after the first five minutes, and have the other person talk about himself.*
4. *After ten minutes, ask for volunteers to exchange information about the other person in their group. Again, do not pick the first person. Wait for volunteers.*
5. *The volunteer then talks to others about the person in the group. Each person can take the time to talk about that person.*
6. *Once all of the individuals have completed this exercise, ask what they learned from this experience.*

The leader can gather information from this exercise to add a personal touch to future discussions. This can be done by using student examples or dialogue.

Communication Within An Organization

There are many types of communication practiced daily. We will discuss four types of communication used within an organization: downward, upward (feedback), peer, and grapevine.

1. *Downward communication starts in an organization* from a higher level and works down to the lowest organization level. Rarely is enough information passed downward with this type of communication, but downward communication is important in an organization.

Usually rules, regulations, policies, and other information from upper management are relayed by downward communication. The information provided by upper management can show the chain of command either in a positive or negative manner. This type of communication allows individuals to develop goals, objectives, responsibilities, and duties within the organization.

Without this downward information movement, the employees become confused, insecure, angry, and defensive. These attitudes can lead to dissatisfied employees, rising absenteeism, and employee moral may be negatively affected. Downward communication needs to be clear and understood by the receiver.

2. *Upward communication* also may be called *feedback*. (However, feedback also occurs with the other types of communication.) Feedback allows for the sharing of information between managers, supervisors, peers, and other employees for problem awareness, commitment, cooperation, and sharing ideas and concepts.

How is this done?

There are two major areas to obtain feedback within the organization. The first area is in regular meetings. In these meetings, discussions occur that include status, goals, problems, and solutions. This is done by working together in groups. The second area of obtaining feedback is the individual meeting, either formal or informal, between manager and employee. These individual meetings are held to discuss personal goals and any work problems.

3. *Peer communication* has some basic problems in most organizations. This type of communication stresses interdepartment dialogue. Sometimes department managers and supervisors tend to not want to work together. This structure does not allow for strong and effective communication.

One of the best ways of resolving the communication problems within the peer structure is to provide ways for managers and supervisors to discuss problems freely and openly. A department manager or supervisor who is not part of the problem could lead these discussions.

Communication between peers can be improved by encouraging group discussions or meetings.

4. *Grapevine* is the only type of communication that doesn't follow the organization structure. The grapevine is generally considered by management to be a negative type of communication. It may be negative at times, but the grapevine *does* provide a valuable source of information.

You may want to set up your own grapevine network. There are ways this can be completed simply by following these suggestions:

    a. Keep all channels of information open.
    b. Cultivate all channels of communication.
    c. Be prepared to give information, but know when to keep things to yourself.
    d. Protect your sources of information.
    e. Never use information against others.
    f. Don't play people against one another.

Forms of Communication

We have many different forms of communication that influence our daily lives. We will be discussing only seven forms of communication in this material. (Perhaps other forms can be developed during your discussions.) They are:

1. *Verbal communication* is the most common form of communication. We think of verbal communication as an "informal" way of letting people know us, expressing our feelings or giving directions. Informal communication is what we do daily. "Formal" communication is what we may do in giving a presentation before a group or something that requires a special effort in giving information. However, most of us are not as familiar with formal communication as we are with informal communication.

There are some techniques and methods in formal communication to use in getting your point across. Some, if not all of the techniques and methods, can be used in informal communicating as well. These techniques and methods are:

    a. Develop an outline and rehearse it.
    b. Show enthusiasm for your subject.
    c. Explain technical terms in the simplest way.
    d. Use humor.
    e. Pace your speech rate.
    f. Speak to everyone in the audience.
    g. Maintain eye contact.

Speaking well is a skill that can be developed, and practicing this skill helps in your total development as a manager and supervisor. Use as many opportunities to speak before groups as possible (group meetings, department meetings, etc.). You may find you enjoy speaking in front of these groups.

2. *Active listening* is a skill that is very important in the process of communication. There are some basic techniques to follow when you are actively listening:

    a. Look at the speaker and watch hand gestures as well as facial expressions.
    b. Strive to understand; be open minded and accepting.
    c. Respond by a nod, a smile, or active exchange of ideas and concepts.

d. Listen without making assumptions.

Watching a speaker may help you when you speak in front of groups. It is important for two-way communication to occur, especially active listening.

3. *Written communication* may be tied with verbal communication as to which one is used most. Writing skills are also learned. Some of the rules for written communication are:

    a. Answer "Who," "what," "when," "where," "why," and "how."
    b. Determine your main theme.
    c. Describe the main points.
    d. Rank supporting points.
    e. Use vocabulary appropriate to the reader.

4. *Reading* is especially important in two-way communication. Reading accurately is just as important as writing accurately. Because of the amount of information available to us, you need to learn to skim the material. In the skimming process, you need to look for the main points and mentally file what you can use for further reference. Reading, like other forms of communication skills, can be learned.

5. *Visual communication* requires different skills in learning. The four different vehicles for visual communication are: physical, aesthetic, symbolic, and signed.

In each of these vehicles there are also other forms of communication. The *physical* form uses smell, touch, body motions, tone of voice, and facial expressions. The *aesthetic* form uses painting, music, sculpture, and dancing. The *symbolic* form of communication can be a religious experience or personal status of an individual. Symbolic communication can be confusing, requiring a knowledge of symbolism. Just like other forms of communication, it depends on the sender to provide a picture of what is trying to be expressed. There is an overlap of these different forms of communication, allowing individuals to provide the best communication possible if the forms are clear and direct.

6. *Signs* are yet another form of communication. Signs can be broken into three groups: mechanical, hand, and sign language. These types of signs require a visual receiver and are types of communication that are with us daily.

Think of mechanical signs. What have you experienced in this form? Railroad signs are a good example. How about hand signs? If you are a baseball fan, the coach uses hand signs or signals to inform the runner when and what to do. Sign language is a formal means of communication for a large group of our population. The deaf primarily use this form of communication and, of course, other types and forms of communication.

7. *Extrasensory perception* is still another form of communication that uses another technique or method to communicate. Clairvoyance, telepathy, and psychokinesis are some examples. Clearly, extrasensory perception requires a different level of communication than other forms.

Communication is important for all of us. However, there *are* barriers to honest and direct communicating:

    a. Reprisal from supervisor or peers.
    b. Lack of topic interest.
    c. Educational background.
    d. Personal bias.
    e. Organization structure.
    f. People unaccustomed to communication.
    g. Employee fact distortion (rumors).

Rumors can be a destroying factor for individuals and organizations. It is therefore important to know about rumors and the rumor mill in your organization.

How does a rumor start? The common causes for rumors are a dislike for someone or something; anger directed at a person or organization; and a mistrust or distrust in a person or organization. Therefore, it is very important to give employees the "real story" about organization matters and situations.

Remember — *listen* to your employees, peers, and supervisors.

Can you think of other barriers that affect positive communication?

LEADER:
Write barriers on the chalkboard for the group to take note and use for possible further discussion.

We have discussed the barriers or problems in communication. How do we overcome these barriers? The following list will give you a start:

1. Use direct feedback.
2. Use direct and simple language.
3. Use effective and active listening.
4. Use repetition as needed.
5. Be honest.
6. Let your employees know where they stand.
7. Give credit where credit is due.
8. Let employees participate in the plans and decisions affecting them.
9. Know all of your employees' names and some personal facts (i.e., birthday, children's names, etc.).
10. Use constructive criticism.
11. Be consistent in your actions.
12. Take every opportunity to demonstrate pride in your employees and department.
13. Settle every grievance.
14. Show employees the importance of every job they complete.
15. Be assertive of your rights and the rights of others.

You can use all of these suggestions — or just a few in combination — to provide effective communication with your employees. These ideas for overcoming communication problems apply not only to job-related activities, but also to all daily contacts.

Giving Instructions and Orders to Employees

How do I get the best results when I give instructions to employees?

1. Be sure your instructions are correct for each situation.
2. Be specific about what you want the employee to do and what results you expect.
3. Have the employee repeat the instructions back to you.
4. Be confident and calm in delivering your instructions.
5. Check to see if your instructions are being carried out.
   If an employee willfully refuses your instructions, what do you do?

LEADER:
Ask the group for their answers and display their comments so that all students can use the information for further discussions.

The first thing: *Do not* fly off the handle! Some positive suggestions are:

1. Ask yourself if the instructions were fair.
2. Ask yourself if the correct person was selected to follow your instructions.
3. Ask yourself if you have done your best in determining the cause of the problem.
4. Ask the employee why he refused to follow your instructions.
5. Take the necessary steps to correct the problem.

You may be faced with a disciplinary problem, but do not be quick to penalize, suspend, or terminate. Find out what the problem is and correct it. If the problem is with you or the employee, deal with the problem *now, do not* wait! Talk to the employee calmly, constructively, and privately.

When employees resist your instructions, remove the resistance by:
1. Trying a successful example.
2. Trying a demonstration.
3. Asking questions.
4. Listening.

DECISION MAKING

DECISION MAKING

Generally, individuals have a mental block when making business-type decisions. Part of the mental block is the feeling that somehow business decisions are separate or different from other decisions.

All of us make decisions hourly, daily, monthly, etc. These decisions are made out of habit more than by special process. However, these decisions, at one time, were made by thinking through a series of steps. These same steps are the same ones we have used all of our lives in making personal decisions. We use these same steps in making business decisions.

Process of Decision Making

In making a decision, there is an orderly process that is followed. The process is followed either consciously or subconsciously. Whatever the decision is, we need to make the best possible one from the information we have at the time of making the decision.

The first part of decision making is taking the risk to make a decision; the next part is much easier. The thought process includes:

1. Establishing a reason for making a decision.
2. Prioritizing the reasons for making a decision. (One approach is to determine "wants and needs" in the process.)
3. Determining the different actions to be taken and balancing the benefits between tangible and intangible actions by asking who, what, where, why, when, and how.
4. Choosing the best path based on the information you have at the moment.
5. Exploring possible adverse consequences of the different paths.
6. Deciding the controls, if any, for your final decision.

Take the risk and make your decision. There is more learning, growth, and effect when you are making decisions than not making decisions. So, take the risk and do it.

Obstacles in Good Decision Making

All of us, at times, create obstacles for ourselves in making good decisions. It helps us to see these obstacles clearly so we can make a connection between the decision and its obstacle.

Some of the obstacles in making good decisions are:

1. Fear of making an incorrect decision.
2. Not enough good information.
3. Habit, i.e., "We've always done it this way."
4. Decision making without input from others.
5. Impulsive decision making.

Overcoming the Obstacles in Making Good Decisions

How do you overcome the obstacles in decision making?

LEADER:
Write the ideas on the chalkboard so all in the group can have them available for discussion.

Some ideas are:

1. Make a conscious decision to overcome the obstacles.
2. Be creative and critical.
3. Involve others in the decision-making process.
4. Gather all information possible.
5. Separate the "good" information from the "bad."
6. Write down the solutions.

Summary

The following nine statements summarize the decision-making process:

1. Establish the reason for making your decision.
2. Classify the reasons by priority.
3. Determine the choices to make the best decision.
4. Choose the best path in making your decision.
5. Explore any possible future problems.
6. Know the effects of your final decision.
7. Review the reasons, problems, or obstacles of your decision-making process.
8. Write down your solutions.
9. Follow up to see if your decision is acceptable or not.

PROBLEM SOLVING

PROBLEM SOLVING

A natural topic to follow decision making is problem solving because a part of problem solving is making decisions. The place to start in solving a problem is to first determine if a problem is present.

Webster's New Collegiate Dictionary defines a problem as:

1. A question of inquiry, consideration, or solution.
2. An unsettled question.

Can you come up with your own comprehensive definitions of a problem?

The Problem-Solving Process

There are five elements in the problem-solving process:

1. Awareness of Problem

This element is affected by many internal and external forces that include: education, peer pressure, information, assumptions, and people involved in the process.

2. Identification of Problem

We ask, "What is the real cause of the problem?" We must go past the symptoms to the real cause. Looking for the cause of the problem takes time and may be costly. But most important, we must be aware of incorrect assumptions in resolving the problem.

3. Investigation of the Problem

Investigate the real problem by asking: Who? What? Where? Why? When? and How? Investigate the real problem without applying incorrect assumptions.

4. Offering Possible Solutions to Problem

Don't stray from the problem, nor try to limit the scope of solutions. In the solution process, determine different paths and analyze the choices. Then decide on the best choice.

5. Decision Making

"How do I make a decision?" This may be the question you have when determining the process needed to resolve a problem. The best approach to answering this question is to use the following principles for decision making:

1. Establish the reason for making your decision.
2. Classify the reasons by priority.
3. Determine the choices for making the best decision.
4. Choose the best path in making your decision.
5. Explore any possible problems that may appear in the future.
6. Know the effects of your final decision.
7. Review the reasons, problems, or obstacles in your decision-making process.
8. Write down your decisions.
9. Follow up on your decision.

Two possible methods to be used in the decision-making process include:

1. Brainstorming — This method and technique is used when there is a small group of less than 10 individuals with a limited amount of time. This approach allows each individual to provide input, and allows for the creative energy to flow. A brainstorming session needs to be controlled, and allowed to develop for a specified amount of time, approximately 25 minutes.
2. Role Playing — This method and technique is used in stimulating a group reaction or an individual response.

Are there other methods and techniques for gathering information for making a decision? What are some of the difficulties encountered in problem solving? What are some of your ideas?

LEADER:

Write the students' suggestions and answers on a chalkboard so the comments will be visible to all the people in the group. Don't forget to include the cause-and-effect diagram as a tool for gathering information, and here is a list of some of the difficulties you may not have discussed:

Jumping to conclusions
Problem is not defined
Emotions get in the way
Lack of information
Incorrect information
Irrelevant data
Pinning blame
Attacking the symptoms rather than the cause of the problem
Inflexible leanings
No system in use in approaching any problem or solution
Bias

The Task Force

An efficient — but more elaborate — alternative in the problem-solving process is the establishment of a task force. The purpose of a task force is to gather information about a problem or proposal, conduct an in-depth examination, and come up with concrete recommendations and/or solutions based on available data.

How do you go about putting together a task force?

Ask yourself: Does your manager want or need you to conduct an investigation? How about making important decisions and recommendations? How are you going to work in the organization? Are you going to train key managers so they will support the task force?

In starting the task force, you need to know the goals and objectives. Put a list of possible goals and objectives together and ask your manager to review your list. Both of you should go through the list and choose the ones that may or may not apply.

There are other important questions that need to be addressed before the task force actively starts. Some of those questions may be:

1. Will individuals be assigned part time or full time to the task force, and how many individuals will be needed?
2. What is the deadline?
3. Do you have a budget? If so, how much?
4. What information will be available to you and the task force?
5. Are reports expected from your task force?

For the task force to function, you need people. They should:

1. Have knowledge and skills relevant to the task force's goals and objectives.
2. Be interested in the project and the task force.
3. Have the time to work in the task force.
4. Enjoy working on projects and with people.
5. Be team members who are not controlling and dominating.

Each person selected for your task force should be personally contacted by you, and there should be a meeting with each individual and his or her manager.

Now you are ready to start — but not so fast! Prepare for your first meeting by reviewing the goals and direction of the project. You should rely on your leadership skills by:

1. Establishing the ground rules for the task force meetings.
2. Making each person feel a part of the group.
3. Making the discussion visual by writing the opinions and thoughts on a chalkboard so all can refer to the material.

4. Bringing out opinions and thoughts from all members.
5. Building on areas of agreement, and then working on the differences.
6. Dividing the group into subgroups as needed.
7. Keeping the meeting moving.
8. Not aligning yourself with any subgroup within the task force.
9. Monitoring and reporting group progress.
10. Publishing minutes of all meetings.

After your goals and objectives are met, how do you *end* the task force? Usually a task force is finished when a summary report is issued to top management of its findings. Then a functioning group within the organization is given the job of working on the task force recommendations.

We have explored the definition of a problem. We have determined and discussed the five elements of problem solving and possible difficulties. Now, let us explore, determine, and discuss problem prevention.

Problem Prevention

Problem prevention can be called *corrective action*. There is a set of eight steps to problem prevention:

1. Have a plan of action.
2. List the steps of your action plan.
3. Isolate the major steps in your plan.
4. Ask, "What could go wrong with my action plan?"
5. Set priorities, or provide a list of possible problem areas.
6. Ask, "What could cause the problem?"
7. Take preventive measures on the causes of the problem.
8. Plan the action: Who? When? Where? and How?

Decision making and problem solving are not mystical. We make decisions and solve problems daily. Still, the supervisor or manager who knows which decisions to make and realizes the limitations of his own problem-solving ability will be more effective as a leader.

Practicing decision-making and problem-solving skills is important. The following case study gives you an opportunity to improve and strengthen your skills in making decisions and solving problems.

> *LEADER:*
>
> *Divide students into small groups. Have each group discuss the case and answer the questions provided. Once the groups have completed this part of the case, have one person in each group discuss the group's answers to the case questions with the rest of the class.*
>
> *This is an open-ended case. The main objective is to follow the decision-making and problem-solving techniques and methods discussed in this chapter.*

CASE STUDY: DECISION MAKING AND PROBLEM SOLVING

Fred Wilkes, supervisor of the pattern room for Bronze Company, is walking back to his desk with a frown on his face. "Gee," he says to himself, "who would have thought that Charlie would get to be the biggest problem I have?"

Charlie Zelder is a drafter from the old school, and Fred had felt lucky picking up such a skilled worker. But Charlie hadn't been around very long before it was obvious that he had his faults as an employee. He was crotchety and fussy. His tools had to be set up in just the right order. He wouldn't work on rush jobs, and he obviously didn't approve of his coworkers.

Over the years, Fred felt that Charlie's good points as a drafter overshadowed his petty gripes and complaints. In the last year, however, Charlie had become harder than ever to get along with. One day he'd complain because someone opened the windows and let in a draft. The next day he'd make a fuss because the engineering department asked for a change that wasn't on the original print. Today Charlie said the lighting was so poor it gave him a headache.

Day by day, Fred is beginning to lose his patience with Charlie. Charlie's talents would not be so hard to do without as they would have been three years ago. There were now several drafters who could do as quality of job as Charlie, and they were easier to get along with.

Fred has finally had enough. "I've made up my mind," he says nodding his head. "The next time Charlie gets out of line, I'm going to tell him just what I think."

Case Questions

1. Why do you think Charlie has gotten to be so difficult to work with, or do you think he has always been difficult?
2. What do you think of Fred's decision?
3. How do you think Charlie will react when Fred tells him what he thinks?
4. If you were Fred, how would you handle Charlie?
5. What decision-making and problem-solving elements did you utilize while working through this case?

MOTIVATION

MOTIVATION

One of the major questions confronting American and foreign business is, "How do we help motivate the individual worker?" The problem of motivation is being discussed and written about in different circles from the Peoples Republic of China to the manufacturer and retailer in the United States. To examine motivation, we will be discussing topics that will take us from motivation to participative management.

The first area of discussion is how we view motivation. For the most part, motivation is seen as something mysterious, but if we view motivation from the perspective that it occurs within each person and is "why people do the things they do," we can start to unravel the mystery.

To help us with the issue of motivation, we will look at a survey conducted in the 1970s by the U.S. Department of Labor involving management personnel, their employees, and the work of three behavioral scientists.

The survey that was conducted involved 25,000 managers and 100,000 employees. The question the individual employees were asked was, "What causes people to do what they do?" The participants of the survey were instructed to list ten responses in order of importance, with number one being the most important. The employees' responses were:[1]

1. Appreciation of work.
2. Making a contribution at work.
3. Sympathetic help on personal problems.
4. Job security.
5. Good pay.
6. Interesting work.
7. Promotion and growth.
8. Company loyalty to its workers.
9. Good working conditions.
10. Tactful discipline.

The managers were instructed to complete the survey and respond to how they felt the employees answered the question. The managers responded as follows:

1. Good pay.
2. Job security.
3. Promotion and growth.
4. Good working conditions.
5. Interesting work.
6. Company loyalty to its workers.
7. Tactful discipline.
8. Appreciation of work.
9. Sympathetic help on personal problems.
10. Making a contribution at work.

PERSONAL MOTIVATION EXERCISE

Directions: Now, rate the following factors as they apply to you. List the ten items in order of importance, with number one being the most important and number ten the least important.

The factors are:

_____ Good working conditions
_____ Making a contribution at work
_____ Job security
_____ Promotion and growth
_____ Good pay
_____ Company loyalty to workers

_____ Tactful discipline
_____ Appreciation of work
_____ Sympathetic help on personal problems
_____ Interesting work

LEADER:
Starting with the first factor and continuing down the list, tally how many students selected each factor as being the most important and the least important. Promote further discussion about the other factors as well.

The basic conclusions from this study are that managers do not know what motivates the general work force, much less their own employees. In order to resolve this and other problems, managers need to investigate what the needs and desires are of their employees and themselves as individuals. Like the exercise that you just completed, not everyone is stimulated by the same items.

The data from this exercise can be used to provide valuable information to start unraveling the mystery of motivation. In searching for the clues of motivation, we find it very important to analyze the information in this exercise. We can then answer the questions, "How do we help motivate the individual worker?" and "What are the rewards?"

Many managers have the opinion that we motivate people by using money as the only stimulation for task completion.

Misconceptions About Motivation

First, managers have the misconception that only one item will cause people to accomplish tasks. As we discovered from the exercise just completed, not all people are motivated by one stimulus. Second, money may be a motivator for some people, but it is a temporary satisfaction. We need more lasting rewards to reinforce positive conditions in the work place.

An experienced manager or supervisor can see that once money is used to stimulate the employee, and once the money has been given, the average employee will improve his habits. Then, in time, performance will taper off. This is followed by another money stimulus and another employee performance increase. This condition occurs if money is the only motivator.

Furthermore, when the economy spirals downward, individuals become concerned about their basic needs. Employees view themselves differently on the job, etc. When the economy spirals upward, individuals have a more relaxed feeling about their jobs and about themselves. Their focus changes when the economy is up as well. The condition and environment affects how employees feel and what they need. As a manager or supervisor, you need to be aware of individual needs and wants and be aware of any economic changes.

Behavioral Scientists

We turn to three behavioral scientists to provide us with the background for producing more permanent and satisfying rewards. A. H. Maslow is the first behavioral scientist we will consider. Maslow developed the "Hierarchy of Needs" involving the concept of physical and emotional concerns based on human needs.[2] The structure used to explain his needs concept is a pyramid design. (See Figure 1 below.) The bottom of the pyramid represents the basic human needs. This basic level includes food, clothes, shelter, water, etc. The second level represents the security that humans need. The third pyramid level is the social need of humans. This level represents love and the need to be part of a group. The fourth level represents ego. This need reflects the feeling of being respected and being important. The fifth and last pyramid level represents self-actualization. This level is the need to do the work you want to do. Furthermore, individual needs change often, fluctuating from one level to another, moving up and down the pyramid. A change can occur hourly or daily, and change can occur from one level to another at the same time. An extreme and rapid change from self-actualization to the very bottom of the pyramid indicates a very real concern for the basic needs in life.

Frederick Herzberg is the second behavioral scientist we will consider. Herzberg's studies were conducted with relation to these motivational factors:[3]

1. The work or the job assigned needs to be challenging, meaningful, and satisfying.
2. Recognition needs to be made for the job completed.
3. Complete responsibility needs to be given for the work.

Herzberg concluded that motivation is made up of meaningful, job-related factors which help the worker to become motivated.

Douglas McGregor's work in management style is also enlightening in unraveling the mystery of motivation. McGregor concludes that management styles are divided into two groups.[4] The first group is the Theory "X" managers. The Theory "X" managers are convinced that people dislike work and will avoid it. They believe employees have little ambition, and that security is very important to them. The second management group is identified as Theory "Y" advocates. This style of management suggests that it is natural to use physical and mental effort in work, as well as in play or rest. The average person learns to seek responsibility under proper conditions. His or her capacity to use imagination, creativity, and ingenuity is used and rewarded. This style of management stimulates employees because it provides a way to challenge human development, allowing for personal achievement, responsibility, and recognition.

We can see that motivation is not mysterious when we can analyze and study human needs and behavior. Important conclusions we can draw about motivation are that:

1. We need to examine the causes of human behavior.
2. We need to treat people as individuals, being aware of personal needs, job direction, and responsibility development.

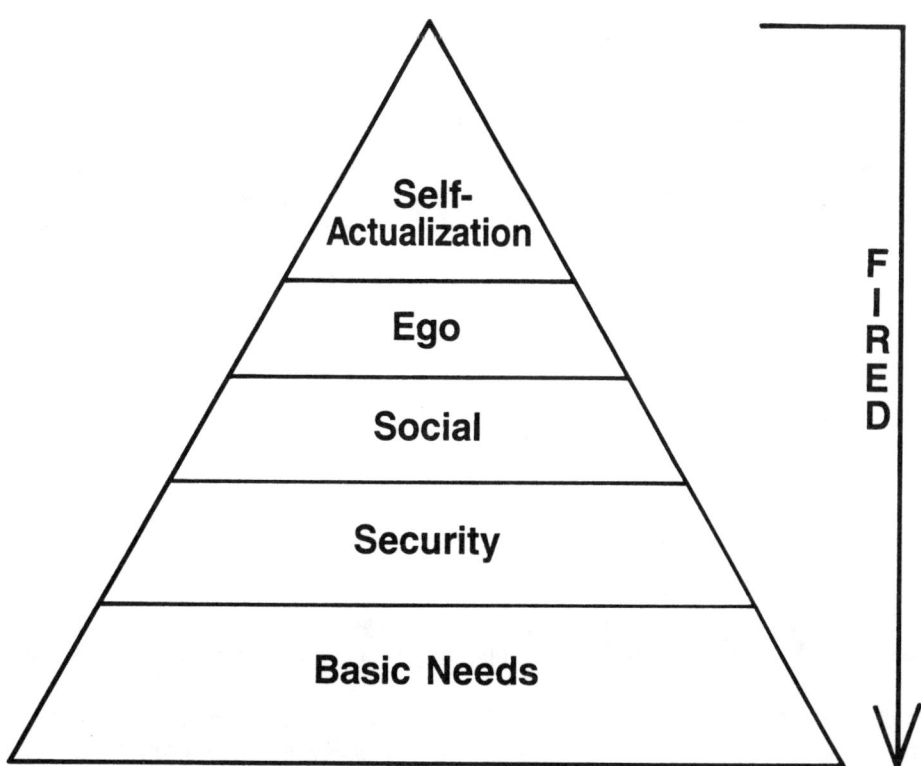

Figure 1. Maslow's Hierarchy of Needs

Motivational Environment

It is important to develop a secure, pleasant environment for motivation to occur in the work place. This type of environment has four basic and important elements:

Trust
Freedom
Honesty
Caring

When the manager and employee achieve these four elements, there is a natural willingness to take on tasks and have a real commitment of purpose. Each element, or the combination of all four, causes motivation to be elevated in most individuals. The reasons for the differences in motivation are the various attitudes, backgrounds, and environments we experience as individuals.

We achieve these elements by developing our skills in:

Communication
Delegation
Planning

These skills become important in establishing the elements of *trust*, *freedom*, *honesty*, and *caring* in the motivational environment. They also provide for individual growth and help form a healthy bond between a manager and employee. This is called *participative management*.

Elements of Motivation

To achieve the basic elements of trust, freedom, honesty and caring, let's speak more directly about communication, delegation, and planning skills or factors. Some of these skills are a review and others are new skills which will be studied more closely in later chapters.

Communication is the first skill to review. Once we know we can stimulate motivation in individuals, we need a communication vehicle to convey information. The vehicle can be one of the many different ways of effective communication.

> LEADER:
> *As a review, list and discuss the different forms of communication:*
> - *Verbal*
> - *Written*
> - *Body motion*
> - *Touch*
> - *Tone of the voice*
> - *Facial expressions*
> - *Painting*
> - *Music*
> - *Dance*
> - *Sign language*
>
> *Ask the students to think of other forms of communication.*

Think of effective communication as being direct, using active listening, using understandable language, being honest, and being actively involved. By applying these communication skills, the normal communication barriers are reduced.

Delegation is the second skill to review. Delegation represents the importance of trusting yourself and your employees by assigning meaningful tasks to complete, allowing the freedom to accept more responsibilities, and giving employees deserved recognition once the task is completed. Delegation further reinforces the motivation factors behavioral scientists concluded in their studies.

Trust and planning are required before the skill of delegation can be achieved. This brings us to the third skill we can review, and that skill is planning.

Planning becomes important when we want to determine direction or action for an individual or organization.

The method for establishing a plan is to first determine what goal you want to accomplish. This is usually stated in general terms such as, "We will reduce defects by 50% by August 1, 1989." Now the goal is translated into the task or objective to be completed. The objective may be stated, "Increase incoming inspections by 90% on critical, major, and minor characteristics by writing each characteristic for every part number to be completed by March 31, 1990."

The characteristics and techniques of a good plan can be weighed by asking: Does the plan work? Is the plan comprehensive? Is the plan worth doing? Is the plan understandable? Is the plan stable and flexible? Is the plan supported by management, employees, and yourself?

To complete the planning process, ask yourself these questions: What elements need to be done? When does each element need to be completed? How is it to be done? Who does the work? Where is the work to be done? What tools or equipment are to be used? What records, if any, will be made? Where and who will record the data? Where will the data be stored? What analysis is required? What feedback is needed? How much time is required? What are the courses of action? What decisions are to be made? What criteria are needed? How is the material going to be identified? How is the material going to be routed?

You may have other questions that need to be addressed, but this is a start. When all of your questions are asked and answered, you have a plan. Further discussion on planning will be made in a later chapter.

In summary, we have determined that trust, freedom, honesty, and caring for the employees are natural factors to motivate willingness in individuals to take on tasks. We have determined that active communication, delegation, and planning are parts of the total picture and help unravel the mystery of motivation. What incentives can you think of that would stimulate your employees or even you?

In general terms, there are two statements that may help. The first statement is to *match individual ambitions to company and department goals*. The second statement is to *find out what each individual wants and show that individual how to get it*.

Since motivation is something which affects everyone, we need to ask, "Why do we do what we do?"

When we look within ourselves, there are three factors which answer the motivation question. They are: *attitude*, *behavior*, and *morale*.

Let us analyze each factor separately.

Attitude. *Attitude* is an individual's expression of feeling, belief, and action toward things, events, or people. A person's attitude is formed through a learning process. Many different events influence an individual's attitude, and part of this learned behavior is reinforced through the years. Since attitude is learned, it can also be unlearned. The unlearning process takes time; it will not occur overnight. If an attitude was learned twenty years ago, it will take some time to be replaced with a new attitude.

Negative and positive attitudes influence the performance of individuals and groups. When individuals decide to act in a particular way to reduce productivity and quality, the supervisor or manager takes action. When dealing with positive attitudes, the supervisor or manager tries to keep the status quo. Only *positive* attitudes need to be reinforced.

Negative attitudes can be changed. We know all attitudes are learned, but what causes an attitude to change from *negative* to *positive*? If it has taken years for a negative attitude to be learned and developed through reinforcement, it will take time and energy on the part of the supervisor and the employee to change the attitude pattern. We may want to make this change in a very short period of time, but remember, it has taken a long time to develop the negative pattern.

One way to make the change is by confronting the individual about his negative attitude. Since an effective manager or supervisor knows the person, he knows what motivates the person. The supervisor can then cause a crisis — something to shake up the pattern within the person. This crisis is followed by reinforcement of the needed change. An example of a crisis would be a demotion or termination. An example of reinforcement would be to *praise* the employee's positive attitude change.

Behavior. Behavior and attitude are related. When we talk about behavior we are talking about the *manner* in which a person conducts himself. Behavior is anything a person does, from involving response or action to a stimulation, to another individual or environment. It can be expressed in terms of *aggressive, nonassertive,* and *assertive behavior.*

Aggressive behavior is when an individual expresses opinions and needs in ways that put down or humiliate the feelings, ideas and the rights of others. Some characteristics of this type of behavior pattern are being direct, domineering at the expense of others, and cutting the lines of communication.

A person engaged in aggressive behavior feels righteous and superior. How do others feel about themselves when one is being aggressive? They may feel humiliated and hurt. How do others feel toward the aggressive person? They feel angry and vengeful. There are certainly other feelings also expressed. Perhaps you can think of more examples.

Nonassertive behavior is when an individual permits himself or others to be put down. The common characteristics of this behavior pattern are being indirect, self-denying, inhibited, and emotionally dishonest. If a person is engaged in a nonassertive behavior pattern, he feels hurt and humiliated. When an individual is being nonassertive, others are feeling either guilty or superior. How do others feel about the person engaged in nonassertive behavior? They feel irritation, pity, and disgust. What other feelings can you think of?

Assertive behavior is expressed when a person stands up for himself in ways that do not violate the rights of others, and he expresses his opinions, goals, and wants in clear, direct and honest ways.

When a person is being assertive, he feels self-worth and confident of his abilities. Others feel valued and respected when a person is assertive. They feel respectful of the assertive person, also.

There are four steps to becoming assertive:

1. Know what you want and ask for it.
2. Accept that you have the right to act.
3. Take action.
4. Be aware of the feelings of others.

What happens when you are and what are your rights? Perhaps you can add your thoughts to the list below.

- Judge your own behavior.
- You are the ultimate judge of yourself.
- You can change your mind.
- You can make mistakes.
- You can say, "I don't know."
- You can say, "I don't understand."
- You can say, "I don't care."

Of course, when we express our rights, we must take responsibility for our actions, whether the consequences are positive or negative.

Morale. The third factor affecting motivation is *morale*. Morale is defined as the mental and emotional condition (enthusiasm, confidence or loyalty) of an individual or group toward a function or task. You may have heard the term *"esprit de corps."* This term is used to describe the feeling of common purpose of a group of individuals, such as United States Marine Corps. The Marine Corps is a good example of a group image with high morale or esprit de corps.

What causes high or low morale in individuals or groups? How are changes made? Factors that can positively or negatively influence morale include:

- Job security
- Interesting work
- Good working conditions
- Appreciation of a job well done
- Recognition
- Good feelings about self
- Media: newspaper, TV, radio, movies, etc.

The manager or supervisor can measure morale in two different ways. The first method is by *observation*. Observations can be made day-to-day in the working environment. The second method of measuring morale is through *morale surveys*. Morale surveys are good only for a specific point in time, while the daily observation of a group's or individual's activities are ongoing and evaluated at different times. The observation method would be the more accurate way for a manager or supervisor to create needed change.

CASE STUDY: EMPLOYEE TURNOVER OR SOME OTHER PROBLEM?

LEADER:
   Have the students work on the case independently, then together in small groups. Discuss the students' answers.

Mary Bassline is manager of the quality control department. She has worked for the organization for five years; during the first three years she was the manager of the purchasing department. This gave Mary a familiarity with most of the raw materials, parts, and supplies used in the organization.

When the manager's job in the quality control department came up, Mary was promoted to it. She was ready and willing to do the best job in her new position. Mary installed some new record-keeping and equipment-issuing procedures. After one year, her department seemed to be in excellent shape.

However, Mary had ten employees working for her when she started, but within a year, six of the ten employees left the organization and needed to be replaced. All six employees had been with the organization for a number of years.

When the personnel manager called this situation to the attention of the plant manager, the plant manager suggested that either an outside consultant be called in or a neutral manager within the organization check into the quality control department and report his findings.

In four weeks, a report was sent to the plant manager from the neutral manager who studied the situation. The findings showed that Mary Bassline was very knowledgeable, and the new methods and procedures she originated were very good. The report stated that the department functioned very well. However, Mary's major weaknesses were in the areas of motivation and communication. Mary seemed to be a very formal person who ran the department with a firm hand. She had created resentment among her employees by taking disciplinary action in public.

After receiving the report, the plant manager wondered what could be done.

Questions to be Answered

1. What options are open to the plant manager and the personnel manager?
2. How is it possible to develop a manager to be a more effective leader?
3. What would be your short- and long-term development plan for Mary Bassline as a manager?
4. If motivation and communication were the only problems, what other skills would Mary need to develop?
5. If you were the personnel manager, would you follow the same course as the personnel manager in this case? If your choices were different, what would they be?

"What Do You Mean I Need to Discipline That Individual?"

Yes, at times you will need to discipline an employee. You may be thinking, "Why did that person break that rule?" or "Why do people break rules?" There are a number of reasons why people break rules, and here are some of them:

- Carelessness
- Noncooperation
- Dishonesty
- Personal problems
- Money problems
- Personal illness
- Family illness
- Lack of initiative
- Lack of effort

Are there others? You may be able to expand this list with other reasons explaining why people break rules. You may find that there are a combination of reasons why rules are broken in your department. Your role as a manager or supervisor is to help the employee adjust to his job and the organization. The goal is to allow the employee to be comfortable in doing the job he is being paid to complete.

A leader has fewer problems when he or she shows a sincere interest in the employees. A good leader is able to provide *positive action* that gets the employee involved in the department, job, and himself. The manager or supervisor who uses constructive criticism, discussions, and listening skills to create change will earn the employees' respect and have fewer problems.

Negative action by a manager or supervisor may be defined as using aggressive behavior to get results. That manager or supervisor may use penalties to get results, but what type of results? How effective is a supervisor's positive or negative action when used toward an employee?

LEADER:
   Use your own experience to determine the answer to this question in class discussion.

There are times when a good manager or supervisor is placed into a position of having to terminate an employee. Termination of an employee is the least desirable and last action to be taken.

There are steps the supervisor can take toward *terminating* an employee. However, company policies for personnel discipline should be checked. Generally, the action steps would be as follows:

   a. A verbal warning is issued the first time someone breaks a rule.
   b. A written warning is issued the second time someone breaks a rule.
   c. The third time, the individual would be terminated.

As managers and supervisors, we need to be sure of our actions and support them with *documentation*. Terminations should be the last possible option to consider.

To be sure of your actions before terminating an employee, ask yourself:

   a. Have I made the company policies clear for disciplining the employee?
   b. Have I documented the clear cut breaking of a rule?
   c. Have I given the employee adequate warnings?
   d. Have I made sure there are no prejudices on my part?
   e. Have I kept adequate records?
   f. Does the punishment fit the infraction?

Can the employee be part of the termination decision through options mutually agreed upon with the supervisor? Consider the following case study.

LEADER:
   Write down the answers to the termination question on the chalkboard, then have the group work on the following case study.

CASE STUDY: PROBLEM EMPLOYEE

Oscar Smithson has been an employee for 15 years with Pitt Manufacturing Company. Oscar has had a number of jobs with the company. He began as a quality engineer and was promoted to quality manager. He had that job for one year when problems started. Oscar insisted that things be done "his way" without regard for how others felt.

Henry Kitz, Oscar's manager, demoted Oscar to quality engineer status and hired Shirley Holms as the quality manager. She had eight years of supervisory and management experience.

Once Shirley started work, more problems with Oscar surfaced. During one of her monthly audits of the inspection records, Shirley discovered that a directive she had given Oscar to communicate to the incoming inspector had not been followed. The directive was to make sure all inspections were recorded in writing and logged in the inspection record book.

Shirley asked the incoming inspector about the directive regarding documentation of records, and the inspector stated, "I never received a directive to write records." Shirley also asked Oscar about the directive, and Oscar replied, "I do not think writing down inspection information is important, and I refused to give the directive to the incoming inspector."

What action steps should Shirley follow to resolve this problem? Remember, termination is the *last option to consider* in resolving a problem.

LEADER:

Some suggestions in answering the questions for this case include the following:

1. *Discuss the problem with the personnel manager.*
2. *Discuss the problem with Henry Kitz and Oscar, separately and privately. Do not overreact.*
3. *Let Oscar know you do not like his actions; that you have nothing against him personally. Let him know that you want to resolve the problem. Shirley may want to offer suggestions, but Oscar will need to make the final decision.*
4. *Develop an action plan that both Shirley and Oscar agree to complete. The action plan may include the following:*
   a. *Document all directives from Shirley to Oscar in a way which requires a written response from Oscar. Both Oscar and Shirley are to receive a copy. Shirley could use this format to determine which memos need answering.*
   b. *Review the progress of Oscar's performance once every 30 days or sooner. Use the memos for the review of Oscar's performance.*
   c. *If these reviews do not resolve the problem, develop a written plan which would include three options agreeable to both Shirley and Oscar.*
      i. *The first option is to maintain a positive work attitude and to complete the tasks per the job description.*
      ii. *If the first option fails, the second option is for Oscar to see the industrial psychologist.*
      iii. *If the second option fails, the third option for Oscar is termination.*

This total plan would need to be in writing and agreed to by both Shirley and Oscar.

Discipline Problem Causes and Suggested Corrective Actions

Each manager and supervisor needs to be aware of why people "do the things they do," and provide corrective action when problems occur.

When a person is dissatisfied and spreads unrest to the rest of the employees, what may be causing the problem? There may be more than one reason for this type of behavior. Some examples may be: work conditions, wages, equipment, leadership problems, handling a grievance poorly, lack of direction, and not enough work. The corrective actions for the problem may include providing detailed work directions, improving the working conditions and equipment, and paying more attention to the employee and his problems.

When employees fool around and waste time, the causes for this problem may be a lack of work or a lack of supervision. The corrective action may include providing better work assignments, paying closer attention to employees, and having personal talks with the employees.

In the following problems, what would be the possible causes and corrective actions for each problem?

1. Tardiness —

   LEADER:
   The possible causes: fatigue, family illness, car problems, or traffic. The corrective action: talk to the employee about the problem.

2. Absenteeism —

   LEADER:
   The possible causes: sickness or personal problems. The corrective action: have a personal talk with the employee and let the employee know that you care.

3. Dishonesty —

   LEADER:
   The possible causes: low wages, severity of discipline, or natural disregard for rules. The corrective action: more supervision, individual attention by the supervisor, and talking to the employee about the problem.

4. Visiting —

   LEADER:
   The possible causes: not enough work, jealousy, or curiosity. The corrective actions: personal talks with the employee, more supervision, and better assignments.

5. Willful disobedience of oral and written directives —

LEADER:
The possible causes: lack of interest, spite, jealousy, or personality conflict. The corrective action: personal attention and talking to the employee.

"Can, I Handle Criticism?"

Yes, if the criticism is constructive.

Every manager needs to evaluate, instruct, and help his or her employees improve. One of the best ways of helping employees is to aid them in strengthening their weaknesses. The "how to" — or feedback — you provide must be tempered to the personality of your employee. Consider your role in discussing problems with employees and providing constructive criticism. Think of what needs to be said and how the employee will take your comments, whether positive or negative.

When giving interviews and appraisals, you need to pick the appropriate place and time. It would be best to choose an informal place for your discussion with the employee. Timing is also important when dealing with the employee. The fact is that you are the "person in charge," or the "boss," and that can be intimidating to your employee even in the best of situations. You can conduct your discussion in a conference room or over lunch at a local restaurant, but your office or organization lunchroom should not be used because of the powerful, intimidating factor, that may make the employee feel uncomfortable.

Once you determine some suggestions to help the employee, discuss them with the individual in general terms, but geared to the specific problem. Use examples to highlight problems or strengths, and propose different ways to overcome the problems or to strengthen performance.

Limit your discussion to only the item or situation that the employee can control and correct. Presenting a situation beyond the employee's control only creates further problems for both of you. Try to strive for a mutual exchange of ideas.

Constructive criticism enables your employees to grow in their jobs, and enables you, the supervisor, to directly affect their growth.

FOOTNOTES

1. Haimann, Theo and Raymond L. Hilgut. *Supervision: Concepts and Practices of Management.* Cincinnati, Ohio: South-Western Publishing, 1977, p. 64.
2. Maslow, A.H. *Motivation and Personality.* New York: Harper & Row, 1954.
3. Fulmer, Robert M. *The New Management.* New York: Macmillan, 1974, pp. 349-354.
4. Haimann, Theo and Raymond L. Hilgut. *Supervision: Concepts and Practices of Management.* Cincinnati, Ohio: South-Western Publishing, 1977, pp. 59-60.

PLANNING

PLANNING

Organizing, staffing, directing, controlling, and planning are the five basic jobs of a manager. Our interest, presently, is in planning. This chapter will deal with planning in more detail than our first brief encounter in the motivation chapter.

We will address these questions: What are the steps in planning? What are the characteristics of a good plan? What are the techniques used in planning?

Steps in Planning

The steps of planning are especially important in determining a general direction. Step number one can be defined as a *goal*. Having a goal is not enough — the goal must be *stated*. Next, *define* the *desired results* of your goal. Once the results are defined, the determination of any subgoals is important. Check to see if your goal is complete before going to step two.

The second step is to determine what new resources are presently available for your plan. Estimate the efforts, programs, and resources already directed to your goal. "Is the plan worth doing?" is important to ask yourself before going to step three.

The third step is to develop possible paths to follow to meet your goal plan. Now, determine different routes for your plan, and select the shortest and best route to reach your goal. New ideas and concepts can be developed along this selected route before proceeding to step four.

The fourth step is to predict possible problems in your goal, such as costs and risks, and to plan for them. These problems would need to be met; detours and hurdles would need to be resolved. The purpose of this fourth planning step is to troubleshoot any potential problems and to eliminate the least workable or practical solutions.

Step number five is to narrow the possible choices of your path by selecting the best way to meet your goal and to plan in general terms.

Step six is building the entire plan. One way to do this is to diagram the selected plan on a piece of paper. During this process, highlight the critical elements of your plan in this visually explicit, diagram format.

The seventh and final step is to critique and follow up any loose ends to make sure your plan is complete.

Characteristics of a Good Plan

There are ten characteristics in determining a good plan. Make sure your plan is:

1. Workable.
2. Comprehensive.
3. Understandable.
4. Properly timed for acceptance.
5. Worth doing: costs, advantages, etc.
6. Stable and flexible.
7. Compatible with present systems and with the organization.
8. Optimized.
9. Self-controlled.
10. Supported by management, peers, and employees.

Techniques of Planning

Techniques are needed in the development of the planning cycle. These planning techniques are best asked as detailed questions to ensure a complete, well-rounded plan. To determine the details of your plan, ask yourself the following questions.

- What elements need management consideration?
- What needs to be done to each of those elements?

- When does each element need to be completed?
- How is it to be done?
- Who does the work?
- Where is the work to be done?
- What tools or equipment are to be used?
- What records, if any, will be made?
- Who will record the data?
- Where will the data be stored?
- What analysis is required?
- What feedback is needed?
- How much time is required?
- What are the courses of action?
- What decisions are to be made?
- What criteria are needed?
- How is the material going to be identified and routed?
- Are there alternative courses of action to be taken?
- What is the time limit required?

Many organizations require a plan for a particular time frame. Normally, the long-range plan is for five years. A sample of an outline and an actual five-year plan follow. The five-year plan in this case is not based on this particular Quality Control Plan Outline.

LEADER:

This exercise can be a written assignment or completed during class time with oral participation by the students. Using the outline below, ask the students to develop answers to the questions contained in the above section, "Techniques of Planning."

For example, tell the class that you have selected under "I. System outline/A. Incoming Inspection" the element "6. Material audits" as an element that needs management consideration. Ask the students to come up with a hypothetical reason about why it needs attention and what needs to be done. Next, move on to the question "How is it to be done?", and so on and so forth.

*Repeat this exercise several times using different elements, and request that the students use the **exact verbiage** that would be appropriate for inclusion in the plan itself.*

Example of a Quality Control Plan Outline

I. System Outline
    A. Incoming Inspection
        1. Sampling plans
        2. Instructions
        3. Data recording
        4. Reporting
        5. Specifications
        6. Maintenance
        7. Calibration
        8. Material audits
        9. Personnel requirements
    B. In-Process and Final Inspection
        1. Sampling plans
        2. Instructions
        3. Data recording
        4. Reporting
        5. Specifications

      6. Maintenance
      7. Calibration
      8. Material audits
      9. Personnel requirements
   C. Material Disposition
      1. Identification
      2. Requests for deviation
      3. Routing
   D. Laboratory Testing
      1. Test specifications
      2. Samples for the laboratory
      3. Requests for tests
      4. Laboratory result reports
II. Vendor Relationships
   A. Quality requirements given to the vendors.
   B. Correlation of measurement methods
   C. Vendor quality capabilities
   D. Material and vendor rating
   E. Feedback
   F. Corrective actions and follow-up
   G. Certification of material and service
III. Process Control
   A. Sampling plans
   B. Analyzing manufacturing processes
   C. Process analysis
      1. To determine capability
      2. To determine the degree of conformity to planned values
      3. To determine cause and effect of variation
      4. To identify cause and effect of nonconformance

Example of a QC/QA Five-Year Quality Plan

Introduction

This five-year development plan gives each plant's Quality Control/Quality Assurance Departments a common direction. The common direction unfolds to a total Quality Assurance organization and program. To achieve this goal, an avenue needs to be established, allowing the Quality department to grow and mature at a similar rate as the company.

The growth and maturity patterns would be controlled assuring they would not be counterproductive to the corporate goals and objectives. They would need to be flexible enough to benefit each plant, and progress at different rates to meet individual expectations. At the end of the five-year planning period, the final results would apply to all plants.

To achieve the results of a total Quality Assurance Department, four categories need to be considered and elaborated. The four categories are: Philosophy, Human Resources, Material Resources, and Costs.

Philosophy

Presently, our quality program meets the basic requirement of a Quality Control Department. The goal, however, is to move philosophically to a Quality Assurance Department. This shift in direction would establish a communication line to measure and analyze each activity and to provide corrective action for each function. The responsibility of the department would include the accepting or withholding of goods and finished products as the result of a measuring and analyzing task.

Emphasizing Quality Assurance would include the following points:

— Provide management tool for decision making by the use of proper communication skills.
— Provide preventive attitude toward quality problems.
— Provide creative function within the organization structure.
— Provide communication that all quality and marketing activities are consistent with each customer's expectations.
— Provide for maximizing employee cooperation to reduce conflict, overlap, rework and scrap, and general waste.
— Provide understandable standards, procedures, and processes.
— Provide responsibility for the quality awareness of the organization.
— Provide a communication function within the organization.

The labor or appraisal activities by Quality Assurance personnel would be minimized. The operators in the different manufacturing, engineering, and other departments would be responsible for the product quality in their individual areas. Automatic inspections by machines and equipment will take on a larger role in the inspection process.

The role of Quality Assurance would use a new auditing and training technique to verify the quality of our products and finished goods. Q-Teams would conduct Quality Assurance's auditing function through a random selection process designed to meet department or product requirements and needs.

The Q-Teams would examine processes, procedures, equipment, methods, techniques, training, and would look for results through a "total view" concept. Recommendations and suggested corrective actions would be made by the Q-Teams during and after each audit. In order for this program to function efficiently, the use of trained personnel would be of paramount importance. This program would be expanded to all other operations within the company family.

Quality Assurance would have ten jobs divided into many separate functions to round out the department. These jobs and functions are: preproduction evaluation; product and process quality planning; purchased material quality planning; evaluation and control; product and process evaluation; quality reporting; measuring equipment; training; post production service; special quality studies; and management.

The two primary objectives in Quality Assurance would be the reduction of inspection by Quality personnel and the increase of analysis work by our Quality staff.

In order to achieve these objectives, we must have our suppliers conducting final inspections before shipping to us. The results of final inspection data would reduce the amount of labor in our incoming function by 85% as well as possibly cutting two to three days out of our present receiving and inspection procedures. Of course, our Quality personnel must be able to supply our purchasing department and each of our suppliers with individual ratings. This type of information is labor consuming. The gathering of data and reports would be available without increased labor costs by using correct, personal computer programming or by using our updated computer system.

Human Resources

During this five-year plan, our human resource levels are based on our plants' current employee needs, projected sales, and company direction. In our home plant, we presently have seven people in the Quality Department. In fiscal 1986, one of our Senior Quality Control Inspectors is retiring. The plan is not to replace this person. However, we do have a need for a part-time clerk. The clerk could handle all of the data collection and reporting duties presently handled by our higher-paid personnel. In 1988, if the work load justifies such an action, the clerk position could be moved to a permanent status.

In 1990, the entire company quality structure could be led by a Director of Quality. This individual would have the responsibility for the quality operations in all the plants and would provide a corporate function. This individual would provide the general leadership in all of the plants, with each plant having a manager, subordinates, and technician functions.

One outlying plant presently has two inspectors. In 1986, there would be a need to add a technical person in the quality function. The additional person would be a quality engineer, who would have the ability to make quality decisions in the plant. In 1988, a technician would be needed; in 1989 a quality manager position would be added. A senior quality technician position would be added to round out the department and to add additional expertise to the plant and department. Individual advancement would be available within the quality structure of this outlying plant. This outlying plant's organization needs to continue as a separate structure from the manufacturing supervisors.

Training is a very important part of our total quality program. We must train our part-time, temporary, and permanent people to do the job right the first time, all of the time.

See Appendices A, B, and C for the personnel and organization charts.

Material Resources

The major effort in the next five years will be computerization for the Quality Department. The computerization of the Quality Assurance files in all plants will be important for keeping pace with our customer demands and for keeping our costs under control. Of course, there will be costs involved with the computerization effort, but they will be able to be justified.

Looking into the future, our customers will be asking for more information about our products. This information will be in the form of test results used for legal and certification purposes. The need for additional knowledge of our products will be another factor in gathering and dispersing accurate information.

The estimated data processing department and outside sources costs would be approximately $15,000. This cost would be offset by our ability to:

— Record each serial-numbered unit and report the test results. This would give us a test record of each unit produced. We could recall inspection data for each part-numbered item for up to ten years.
— Provide supplier performance information. This would help purchasing to distinguish acceptable suppliers from the unacceptable ones. Purchasing would use the information when discussing price and quantity orders.

There would be cost-saving advantages to the company. We would save dollars with a higher quality of received material, as well as a better quality and less costly manufactured unit.

Costs

Nine individuals are directly involved in quality within the two plants. Over the five-year plan, the number of individuals directly involved in quality would be increased to 12. At a minimum, four additional people are needed during the next five years to match our company's present growth pattern. In this plan, the additional staffing is divided between the two plants, with the outlying plant receiving three people and the home plant one person.

The expense budget shows a steady increase in a few accounts each year for both plants. This is due to the planning for inflation and the conservative nature of the plan.

Capital acquisitions are minimal at planned amounts from $8,000 to $33,000 in different years. The planned acquisitions mostly are used for data collecting and storage. With these types of capital acquisitions, the labor costs are to be maintained at low levels while maintaining high levels of technical knowledge, ability and department expertise.

See Appendices D and E for the budgets.

Personnel Needs During The Five-Year Planning Period
APPENDIX A

Home Plant

	86	87	88	89	90
Director of Quality	0	0	0	0	1
Quality Assurance Manager	1	1	1	1	1
Quality Engineer	1	1	1	1	2
Sr. Quality Control Insp./Tech.	1	1	1	1	1
Quality Assurance Technician	3	3	2	2	1
Clerk	½	½	1	1	1
Employees Requested Total	6½	6½	6	6	7

Outlying Plant

	86	87	88	89	90
Quality Manager	0	0	0	1	1
Quality Engineer	1	1	1	1	1
Sr. Quality Technician	0	0	0	0	1
Quality Technician	2	2	3	3	2
Employees Requested Total	3	3	4	5	5

Present Organization Chart
APPENDIX B

Home Plant

```
                    ┌──────────────┐
                    │    Q.C.      │
                    │   Manager    │
                    └──────┬───────┘
            ┌──────────────┴──────────────┐
            │                      ┌──────┴───────┐
            │                      │  Associate   │
            │                      │  Qual. Eng.  │
            │                      └──────┬───────┘
      ┌─────┴─────┐           ┌───────────┴──────────┐
  ┌───┴────┐  ┌───┴────┐  ┌───┴──────┐        ┌──────┴───┐
  │  Sr.   │  │  Sr.   │  │Technician│        │Technician│
  │Inspector│ │Inspector│ │          │        │          │
  └────────┘  └────────┘  └──────────┘        └──────────┘
```

Outlying Plant

```
            ┌──────────────┐
            │    Plant     │
            │Superintendent│
            └──────┬───────┘
        ┌─────────┴─────────┐
   ┌────┴────┐         ┌────┴────┐
   │Inspector│         │Inspector│
   └─────────┘         └─────────┘
```

Proposed Organization Chart
APPENDIX C

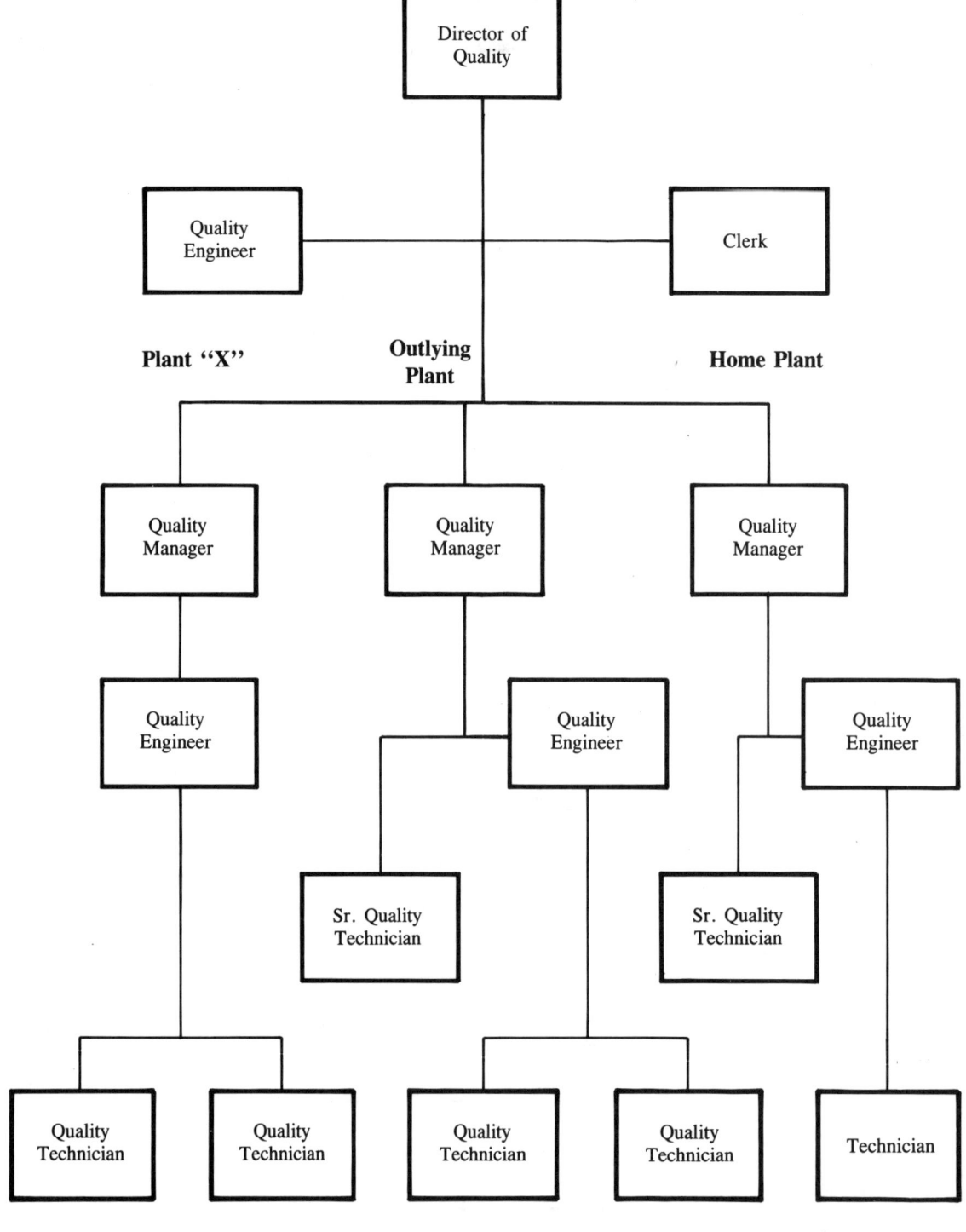

Material Resources For The Home Plant
APPENDIX D

Expense Budget

	86	87	88	89	90
Shop Supplies	1,000	800	800	800	800
Tool Expense	2,000	2,200	2,200	2,200	2,200
Office Supplies	3,000	3,200	3,300	3,400	3,500
Equipment Repair	2,000	2,000	2,000	2,000	2,000
Professional Services	500	500	500	500	500
UL & CSA Testing	700	700	700	700	700
Lodging	400	400	400	400	400
Meals	400	400	400	400	400
Transportation	3,000	3,000	3,000	3,000	3,000
Business Meetings	100	100	100	100	100
Seminars & Education	2,000	2,100	2,300	2,400	2,500
Dues & Subscriptions	500	500	500	500	500
Total Expense	15,600	16,200	16,600	17,100	17,500
Wages	163,542	173,982	158,648	166,648	179,976

Capital Budget

	86	87	88	89	90
Environmental Chamber	9,000				
Vibration Tester	5,000				
Torque Calibration	2,000				
Board for Honeywell Recorder	1,000				
Scale	2,000				
Borescope	2,000				
Data Logger	4,000		4,000	4,000	
Dynamic Port. Harness Tester	6,000				
IBM PC and Software		7,000			
Spring Tester		10,000			
Calibration Equipment		4,000			
Circuit Bd. Component Tester		10,000			
Infrared Thermometer		2,000			
Optical Comparator			20,000		
Load Bank — Laboratory, Q.A.				6,000	
Paint Testing Equipment				3,000	
Metal Analyzing Equipment				5,000	
Computer Assisted Test Equip.					30,000
Total Capital	31,000	33,000	24,000	18,000	30,000

Material Resources For The Outlying Plant
APPENDIX E

Expense Budget

	86	87	88	89	90
Shop Supplies	600	600	600	600	600
Tool Expense	3,000	3,200	3,300	3,400	3,500
Office Supplies	2,000	2,200	2,300	2,400	2,500
Equipment Repair	100	100	100	100	100
Professional Services	100	100	100	100	100
UL & CSA Testing	700	700	700	700	700
Lodging	100	100	100	100	100
Meals	100	100	100	100	100
Transportation	1,000	1,000	1,000	1,000	1,000
Business Meetings	-0-	-0-	-0-	-0-	-0-
Seminars & Education	1,000	1,000	1,000	1,000	1,000
Dues & Subscriptions	200	200	200	200	200
Total Expense	8,900	9,300	9,500	9,700	9,900
Wages	43,829	46,021	63,459	86,596	88,404

Capital Budget

	86	87	88	89	90
Height Gage	1,000				
Load Bank Tester	8,000				
Electronic Tester	1,000				
Gloss Meter		2,000			
Paint Test Equipment		3,000			
Calibration Equipment		4,000			
IBM PC and Software			7,000		
Scale			2,000		
Bore Scope			2,000		
Torque Calibration Tool			2,000		
Data Logger			4,000	8,000	
Computer Assist Test Equip.					30,000
Total Capital	10,000	9,000	17,000	8,000	30,000

TIME MANAGEMENT

TIME MANAGEMENT

Our lives revolve around two gods — the clock and time. From the time we are born until our deaths, the clock and time are important to us. Look how our lives are arranged. First, we awaken to the sound of an alarm clock. Second, a bell may start and end our day at work. Third, a click of the light switch, and we go to sleep.

Do you feel in control of your life? Is your desk top so full of paper and other items that you have no idea where to start?

Try this exercise. Using a pencil take a piece of paper and divide the paper vertically into eight spaces. Now divide the paper horizontally into sixteen spaces. You now have a grid. Across the top of the eight spaces left to right write the time in the first space, and follow that with the days of the week (Monday, Tuesday, Wednesday, Thursday, Friday). Now in the horizontal spaces, under the word time, divide your days into time slots.

For one week use the grid to determine just what you do during the sixteen time slots. This exercise may be full of surprises for you and help you to answer questions such as:

Where and on what do you spend your time? Do you want more time to do other tasks?

You can organize your time to make some sense for what you do and want to do on a daily and weekly basis. To help you with the organization of your time, the following suggestions may be beneficial:

- Group similar activities.
- Use the telephone instead of your feet.
- Do difficult items first.
- Take periodic rests.
- Do big jobs in little pieces.
- Do trivial items at one time.
- Avoid stressful activities in the latter part of the day.
- Create a quiet time and place for yourself.
- Have a set time to leave work.
- Let others help.
- Delegate.

Of course, you may have others telling you what to do about putting your day in order. The responsibility however is yours — do it!

Management By Objectives (MBO)

Management By Objectives (MBO) is a planned and organized approach to direct you, your department, and company to move in one direction. In moving in concert, the first part of the MBO plan is to establish a goal or a series of goals. The goal is usually stated in general terms.

A goal should be achievable through the use of objectives. Also, goal setting needs to meet the individual employee's own ability and needs to help increase production, promote good morale, and provide for good communication.

Objectives are stated in detail and in measurable terms. You can think of objectives in the same manner as goals, but with some important differences.

The differences are:

1. Each objective is viewed as an independent thought, function, or operation.
2. Each objective is measurable.
3. Each objective has an agreed-upon completion date.

Practice at goal setting and objective writing allows for an easier time of going through the MBO process. In each organization the goal setting and objective writing may be different, but the end result is the same. The individual, department, and organization working in concert to achieve the goals.

The following goals and objectives are examples for a Quality Control Department. However, you can use them for developing goals and objectives for any department within an organization.

Example of Quality Control Goals and Objectives
FISCAL 1986

I. Organization development
   A. Quality laboratory
      1. Develop and design a test bank to combine circuit boards, rectifier plates, coils, breakers, and other miscellaneous testers. Recommend an action and build plan.
      2. Develop and design a tester to use on coils so that each coil winder could test his coils. Recommend an action and build plan.
      3. Maintain a laboratory work schedule for testing and analysis.
   B. Human resource development
      1. Develop career plans for "key" people in the department.
      2. Develop performance plans with each person in fiscal 1986.
II. Product quality improvement
   A. Quality costs
      1. Develop assembly procedures for the different operations in both plants.
      2. Continue to report monthly the rework, scrap, and returned goods that are controlled by quality control.
         a. Data supplied to each department by actual and goal.
         b. Data supplied to each department by number of rejections per month.
   B. Manufacturing quality
      1. Develop computer programs for problem-solving and decision-making analysis.
      2. Develop the assembly procedures with computer assistance to reduce errors.
      3. Establish a production supervisor evaluation board to review rejections, rate of quality percentages, and communication of quality.
      4. Establish controls on rework and scrap.
         a. Review quality control data in charging of scrap.
         b. Review methods and techniques for the control of rework and scrap.
      5. Establish a task force to review scrap and rework causes and resolve the problems.
      6. Conduct training in the principles of individual quality for all new employees.
      7. Conduct training in quality philosophy for all employees.
   C. Quality control product audits
      1. Follow the written procedures for conducting line audits.
      2. Conduct random warehouse audits per written procedures.
      3. Conduct quarterly executive audits during fiscal 1986.
      4. Conduct sales department review of product quality on a regular basis.
      5. Complete formal reports and corrective action on each audit.
III. Other plants
   A. Maintain a watch on training needs and wants.
   B. Maintain a team from the quality staff to support the other plants.
   C. Provide quality audits of the quality program in the other plants, to be conducted at random and quarterly bases.
IV. Quality image
   A. One (1) visitation in the field with sales personnel and customers by the quality staff during the fiscal year.
   B. Regularly scheduled meetings with sales department personnel and customer service personnel to discuss problems and corrective actions.

C. Regularly scheduled meetings with engineering personnel to discuss new and present design, projects, documentation, problems, and corrective actions.
V. Budget responsibilities
   A. Develop a fiscal budget for expenditures and capital development for the fiscal year.
   B. Maintain the fiscal budget.
VI. Vendor evaluation
   A. Develop a vendor rating system in conjunction with data processing and purchasing.
   B. Develop a vendor qualification program with purchasing.
   C. Develop a vendor guide for materials evaluation with purchasing.
   D. Develop a program that requires each vendor to provide final inspection data on each lot or batch shipped with the inspection data included in each shipment.
VII. Training programs
   A. Review the training program for employees.
   B. Provide for opportunities for Quality Department personnel to take and complete courses that will benefit the company and the employees in all plants.
VIII. Personal development
   A. Provide leadership and support by being a contributing member of different task force activities and regularly scheduled meetings.
   B. Attend a minimum of one (1) quality control or quality-related conference or seminar in the fiscal year.
   C. Continue as an active member of ASQC by meeting attendance and, if the opportunity arises, teach one (1) or more evening courses sponsored by ASQC at one of the local schools.
   D. Continue to develop career plan through personal goals and objectives.

ORGANIZING AND THE ORGANIZATION

ORGANIZING AND THE ORGANIZATION

As a manager, you need to establish your department's direction or goal, as well as your authority and responsibility limits. Some recommendations for managers are:

1. Let your department become a management tool.
2. Develop a preventive attitude so your department may be viewed as a creative group and part of the management team.
3. Communicate that your department activities coincide with the organization's purpose.
4. Organize your department to maximize and utilize individual resources to reduce waste, conflict, and overlap.
5. Don't let your Quality Control/Assurance Department become the "police force" for all other departments.
6. Don't build an "empire" by excessive control of all activities.

So how do I go about organizing my department? There are three areas that are important in organizing a department. The first area is the *planning period*. This planning period reflects a series of basic questions based on what, when, why, who, where, and how that need to be answered.

These questions are best stated as follows:

1. What is the job to be done?
2. When is the job to be completed? (This is the timetable for your department's development.)
3. Why is the job necessary? (This is the justification for your department.)
4. Who is going to be responsible for getting the job done?
5. Where is the job going to be completed?
6. How is the job going to work?

The second area to discuss is the *loop-closing period*. This part of the organization is the fine tuning of the department that closes the loop in making decisions, and provides corrective action. This occurs through the following steps:

1. Plan the job by the method or procedure.
2. Provide tools to complete the job with personnel input and feedback.
3. Perform the job by using: inspection, audits, tests, analysis, etc.
4. Analyze the results of the inspections, audits, and tests.
5. Provide the means to correct or modify the methods and techniques required to do the job correctly.

The *check and balance area* in organizing a department is the third area to consider. This is divided into three parts. The first part is to develop an automatic check and balance system within your department. The second part is to not have one person totally responsible for a complete action. For example, when giving a performance review, the supervisor signs the document, then the manager signs the document. Thus, two levels in the organization become involved in the decision-making process. The third part in the check and balance department organization would be the formation of a small group for controlling the corrective actions of the entire organization, i.e., a materials review board.

There are organizational hazards to be avoided whenever possible. Some ways to avoid organizational hazards include these suggestions:

1. Don't let the chain of command get too long.
2. Keep the number of responsibility levels to a minimum.
3. Don't ask one person to report to two different managers or supervisors.
4. Don't assign a supervisor or assistant who is expected to perform the exact work as the manager.
5. Watch out for unclear job assignments.
6. Don't put responsibilities with conflicting objectives in the same group.

Why are these considered hazards? Can you think of other organizational hazards?

LEADER:
Discuss questions with students.

ORGANIZATIONAL STRUCTURES

There are many organizational structures, but we will be discussing the two major forms. These two forms are *flat* and *tall* structures.

The *flat* organization structure is defined as one person being in charge, having all the responsibility and authority. This type of organization structure is illustrated as follows:

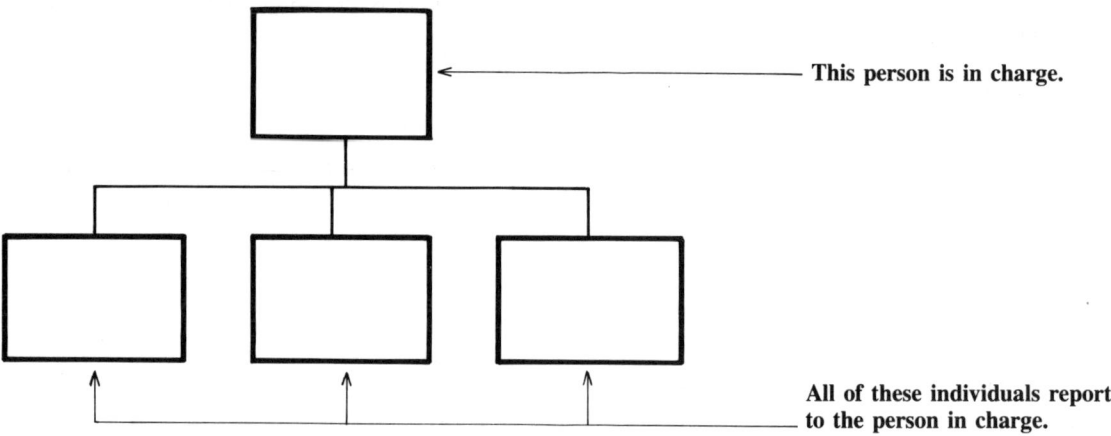

The *tall* organization structure includes many layers of responsibilities and authority. This type of organization structure is illustrated as follows:

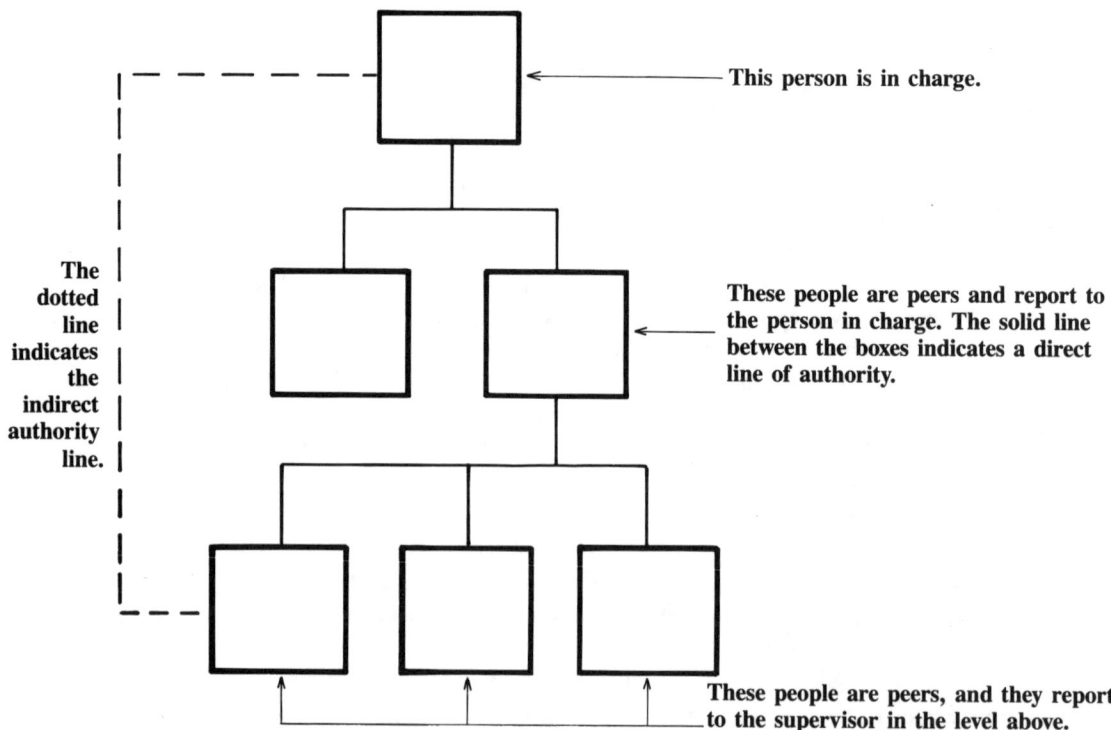

By having an organization chart, you can determine responsibility, function, pay levels, and who is doing what job. The top position on the chart would have the most responsibility and authority, as well as pay. As you move down the organization chart, each level would have less responsibility, function, and pay.

The organization chart is an aid in a department's organizing process. After the department is functioning, the chart would be helpful in providing a model and structure of its operations.

LEADER:
Why not ask the students to draw an organization chart for their respective companies. Depending on the size of the company, the students can draw the organization chart using individual positions or departments. The larger companies might be more easily represented by departments.

Another aid in the organization is the *job description*. This aid spells out the principal duties and functions of the various jobs within the organization. The job description also illustrates the scope and kinds of authority related to each job. The job description is important when reviews are given and is the basis for determining individual performance.

The Purpose of Position Write-Ups

Write-ups, also called job descriptions, define the major areas of accountability assigned to each position so improved individual and positive performance will result. When employees are involved in developing their own job descriptions, they experience a feeling of participation within the organization. Job descriptions also help to define the scope of authority for each position and to whom each employee is directly accountable. Employees develop a deeper understanding with immediate supervisors for position responsibilities and of results that are both expected and needed.

Accurate and up-to-date position write-ups provide an opportunity to improve organizational communications between management and employees. The end result will be an overall better coordinated organizational structure, developed for the benefit of individual employees, supervisors, managers, and the entire organization.

The following position write-ups are examples of a total department's commitment to defining major areas of accountability for individual positions and employees.

POSITION WRITE-UP

POSITION TITLE: Quality Control Manager   DATE: November 1, 1986
DEPARTMENT: Quality Control
ACCOUNTABLE TO: President

PRIMARY OBJECTIVE OF POSITION

To plan, direct, and manage the Quality Control Department in order to provide a product within quality limits established with regard to the performance, physical characteristics, fitness for use, and profit.

MAJOR AREAS OF ACCOUNTABILITY

1. Plans and defines management objectives and achievable goals for the quality control functions that will assure coordinated management efforts needed to achieve the desired level of growth and profitability.

   — Develops, implements, and maintains the Quality Control policy, procedure, and objectives.
   — Meets customer quality requirements, company objectives, and quality control technological state of art.
   — Keeps track of measurements in internal and external failures such as scrap, rework, and returned goods.

2. Directs the quality control functions to provide an acceptable product which meets established requirements of performance, physical characteristics and fitness for use.

- Establishes and maintains inspection test methods and procedures in: incoming, in-process, outgoing, and stored goods.
- Is responsible for budget planning (operational and capital) and maintaining acceptable expenditure levels for the operating expenditures and capital acquisitions.
- Reviews and communicates field complaints and returns for in- and out-of-warranty component and unit problems.

3. Develops and maintains effective and efficient quality systems for vendor performance.
    - Involves Purchasing in planning, implementing, and maintaining vendor-performance programs.
    - Keeps abreast of measurements based on surveys, on-sight inspections, and reported by lots received as accepted and rejected.
4. Participates with Purchasing, Engineering, and Manufacturing in matters involving product quality, product reliability, material standards, and process tool quality capabilities.
    - Coordinates activities, customer satisfaction, and profitability through the Material Review Board, customer surveys, and visitations.
5. Establishes and maintains the necessary quality control documentation to provide adequate history of product manufactured and tested.
    - Monitors completeness, accuracy, and available records.
6. Develops and maintains effective and efficient assignment of responsibility and expected level of performance for assigned employees.
    - Clarity of assignments, organization and flow of work, review and evaluation process, and size and makeup of staff.
7. Provides supervision, guidance, and training for assigned personnel to develop their work potential, prepares them for promotional opportunity, and gives them a sense of job satisfaction and participation in the achievement of company goals and objectives.
    - Growth, ability, attitude and performance of assigned personnel.
8. Evaluates the work performance of assigned personnel on a continuing basis to provide for commendation or to identify need for improvement or change.
9. Keeps the president informed in all matters relating to quality that will help the president function effectively.
10. Provides leadership, through example, for employee attitudes and work habits.
11. Performs other duties as assigned or as required.

Responsibility for work of others

Direct supervision over:
    Quality Engineers
    Quality Technicians
    Quality Control Inspectors
    Senior Quality Technicians
    Quality Assurance Clerk

PREPARED BY: REVIEWED BY: APPROVED BY:

POSITION WRITE-UP

POSITION TITLE: Quality Engineer   DATE: November 1, 1986
DEPARTMENT: Quality Control
ACCOUNTABLE TO: Quality Control Manager

PRIMARY OBJECTIVE OF POSITION

To support and conduct Quality Control/Assurance activities in the development, design, test, and analysis of components and finished products to meet established standards of quality.

MAJOR AREAS OF ACCOUNTABILITY

1. Responsible for the reliability of the manufacturing process.
   — Verifies the manufacturing process.
   — Works with manufacturing to establish new processes.
   — Collects data to assure a stable process.
   — Uses statistical methods (control charts, sampling plans, etc.) to measure the manufacturing process.
   — Establishes the means for controlling the process.

2. Responsible for quality standards, procedures, and process.
   — Writes and examines for accuracy quality specifications and standards.
   — Verifies correct tolerances on drawings and specifications.
   — Writes all quality procedures.
   — Determines the critical, major, and minor characteristics to be followed with costs in mind.
   — Maintains Quality Control/Assurance Department records of tests and reports conducted.

3. Supervision of Quality Department personnel.
   — Reviews individual work and quality of work.
   — Conducts job evaluations.
   — Takes an active role in the development of individual employees.

4. Maintains the quality system at a minimum cost for controlling quality.
   — Works with Design Engineering to assure customer needs are fulfilled.
   — Determines ways and means of testing present and new materials, components, and finished product.
   — Conducts training of inspectors, manufacturing people, sales, customer service, and vendors to implement and maintain the quality program.
   — Assists in the solution of problems in the manufacturing cycle.

5. Responsible for the analysis of data, material, and corrective action, as necessary, to improve systems, procedures, product, and cost.
   — Audits the quality system and makes recommendations for improvements.
   — Determines weaknesses in the manufacturing process and makes provisions for corrective action.
   — Determines scrap and rework costs.
   — Determines methods and techniques to reduce scrap and rework costs.
   — Records and analyzes data.

6. Responsible for the vendor evaluation program.
   — Determines ways and means of testing vendor capabilities (i.e., rating, qualifications, visitations) and maintaining a positive working relationship with them.
   — Works with the Purchasing Department with assistance in vendor relations.

7. Responsible for the calibration of equipment.
   — Controls measuring equipment, both electrical and mechanical, with an acceptable calibration system and program.
   — Maintains the calibration program as modeled in military specification MIL-Q-9858 and other established standards.

8. Keeps work area clean and orderly.

9. Performs other duties as assigned or as required.

Other Job Requirements
- Work involves lifting and handling of different materials, components, and finished product.
- Work involves potential exposure to high voltages from test equipment and finished product.
- Work involves the use of electrical and mechanical measuring equipment.
- Work involves decision making, problem solving, and analysis of test data.
- Work involves a knowledge of blueprints, circuits, and writing reports.
- Work involves conducting tests, making analyses, and writing reports.
- Work involves a knowledge of military standards, specifications, and other working standards and specifications.
- May be ASQC certified as a Quality or Reliability Engineer.
- May have a two (2) year degree or certificate in Quality or in a related area and/or a four (4) year degree in engineering or in a related area.
- Work involves 15% travel.
- Work involves the supervision of Quality Department personnel and provides work direction to the personnel of other departments.

Supervision of:
Senior Quality Technicians
Quality Technicians

PREPARED BY: REVIEWED BY: APPROVED BY:

POSITION WRITE-UP

JOB TITLE: Senior Quality Assurance Technician   DATE: April 5, 1986
DEPARTMENT: Quality Control
REPORTS TO: Quality Control Manager

JOB OBJECTIVE

To conduct, monitor, maintain, and administer tests, inspections, analyses, and audits needed to support the quality objectives and procedures of the company.

DUTIES AND RESPONSIBILITIES

1. Aids in the evaluation of new designs and test laboratory procedures.
2. Tests, analyzes and accurately reports new and present sourced components and products.
3. Approves first piece parts, components, assemblies, and final product from the initial setups in accordance with established quality standards.
4. Monitors, implements, and conducts tests, inspections, and audits for all operations in the manufacturing cycle to established quality standards.
5. Assists in the training of manufacturing and Quality Control personnel.
6. Monitors field complaints and provides timely and accurately written reports to vendors, customers, and management, and recommends corrective action.
7. Conducts life, reliability, and field test programs with all needed follow-up.
8. Tags and initiates disposition of rejected materials, components, assemblies and finished product per established quality procedures and standards.
9. Reviews quality problems as assigned, initiates and recommends corrective actions.
10. Processes scrap, rework, and other rejected items and writes a report on them to quality management.
11. Conducts accurate, complete, and timely calibrations.

12. Develops a positive working relationship with vendors and customers.
13. Maintains the Quality Control Department documentation system accurately and completely.
14. Keeps work area clean and orderly.
15. Performs other duties as assigned or as required.

Other Job Requirements

- Work involves lifting and handling of materials, components, assemblies, and finished product.
- Work involves the use of electrical and mechanical test and measuring equipment.
- Work involves potential exposure to high voltage from test equipment and finished product.
- Work involves a knowledge of blueprints, circuits, electricity, both electrical and mechanical test equipment, schematics, and troubleshooting techniques. Have a Vo-Tech certificate in a related area or work experience in a related area.

PREPARED BY: **REVIEWED BY:**   **APPROVED BY:**

POSITION WRITE-UP

POSITION TITLE: Quality Assurance Technician   DATE: April 1, 1986
DEPARTMENT: Quality Control
REPORTS TO: Quality Control Manager

PRIMARY OBJECTIVE OF THIS POSITION

To carry out Quality Laboratory tests, audits, and inspection activities necessary to support the Quality objectives and procedures.

MAJOR AREAS OF ACCOUNTABILITY

1. Tests, analyzes, and accurately records the electrical and mechanical performance of selected materials, parts, assemblies, and finished products.
2. Tests, analyzes, and accurately records the results of items returned, audits, and inspections referred to Quality Assurance for analysis.
3. Sets up, conducts tests, and operates all quality equipment.
4. Designs and/or assembles test equipment for use in conducting performance and/or life tests on selected products and product components.
5. Provides audits and inspections as needed and assigned in Incoming, In-Process, and Final functions in accordance with established quality standards and procedures.
6. Approves initial test, audit, and inspections in accordance with established quality standards and procedures.
7. Properly documents acceptable or rejected components, materials, and finished products tested and analyzed.
8. Maintains Quality test procedures and other established documentation for completeness and accuracy.
9. Prepares written reports on tests, audits, and inspection results and analysis recommendations for items tested according to quality guidelines for submission to management.
10. Keeps the Quality Laboratory work area clean and orderly for effective use and safety.
11. Performs other duties as assigned or as required.

Other Job Requirements

- Work involves lifting and handling of materials, parts, components, and finished product.
- Work involves the use of electrical and mechanical test equipment, and measuring equipment.

- Work involves potential exposure to high voltage from test equipment and finished product.
- Work involves a knowledge of blueprints, circuits, electricity, and electrical and mechanical test equipment.

PREPARED BY: REVIEWED BY: APPROVED BY:

POSITION WRITE-UP

JOB TITLE: Quality Control Inspector   DATE: February 5, 1986
DEPARTMENT: Quality Control
REPORTS TO: Quality Control Manager

JOB OBJECTIVE

To monitor, maintain, and administer the Quality Control procedures for inspection and testing of raw materials, parts, sub-assemblies, and final assemblies to meet established standards of quality and performance.

DUTIES AND RESPONSIBILITIES

1. Monitors and implements the Quality Control procedures for inspection and testing of raw material, production parts, sub-assemblies, and final assemblies to ensure they meet established standards of quality and performance.
2. Sets up and conducts inspections and tests on raw materials and production parts in accordance with established procedures.
3. Inspects and approves first piece parts from initial setup in accordance with established procedures.
4. Tags and initiates dispositions on rejected materials.
5. Maintains Quality Control procedures and documents in accordance with established procedures for accuracy and completeness.
6. Reviews quality problems as assigned and initiates or recommends corrective action as required for the acceptance, rejection, rework, or other disposition of material.
7. Reports on and processes scrap and reject material.
8. Maintains Quality Control documentation system.
9. Participates on Material Review Board in resolving quality concerns and situations.
10. Maintains current set of prints and procedures for Quality Control.
11. Monitors and reports on problems and discrepancies to minimize scrap and downtime.
12. Performs other duties as assigned or as required.

Other Job Requirements

- Work involves lifting and handling of materials.
- Work involves use of electrical and mechanical test equipment, and measuring equipment.

PREPARED BY: REVIEWED BY: APPROVED BY:

POSITION WRITE-UP

POSITION TITLE: Quality Assurance Clerk   DATE: July 1, 1986
DEPARTMENT: Quality Control
ACCOUNTABLE TO: Quality Control Manager

PRIMARY OBJECTIVE OF THIS POSITION

To accurately perform typing, clerical, and keypunch duties for the Quality Control Department to meet department goals and objectives.

MAJOR AREAS OF ACCOUNTABILITY

1. Responsible for the typing of the department's communication needs.
   — Accurately types documents in accordance with instructions and established procedures.
   — Types department communications in a timely manner.
   — Follows verbal and written instructions and established procedures.
2. Responsible for maintaining department files of documents, drawings, tags, and reports in accordance with established procedures to ensure accurate control and timely availability of department documents.
   — Accurately files all department documents by using established filing procedures, standards, methods, and techniques.
   — Files documents daily (i.e., in-process inspection tags, reject tags, rework orders, etc.).
3. Responsible for the accurate and timely keypunch, collection, and reporting of department data.
   — Daily keypunches accurate department data.
   — Collects data for department reports and reports those data on a regular basis (i.e., Rectifier Plate Report; Line Reject Report; Incoming Report; In-Process Report; Month Report; etc.).
   — Provides department data on a special requirement basis in an accurate and timely manner.
4. Responsible for maintaining military specifications, standards, and index.
   — Keeps in order and maintains the department specification, standard, and index file.
   — Files all specifications, standards, and index following standard filing procedures.
5. Responsible for answering the department telephones.
   — Answers the telephone in a friendly and mature manner.
   — Takes accurate telephone messages as required.
   — Provides accurate and timely response to telephone messages for Quality Control personnel.
6. Keeps work area clean and orderly.
7. Performs other duties as assigned.

Other Job Requirements

— Work involves typing, filing, telephone, and writing skills.

PREPARED BY: REVIEWED BY: APPROVED BY:

JOB DESCRIPTION EXERCISE

You have seen various examples of job descriptions. Now is your chance to create a job description. Identify your present job. (If you do not have a job presently, create the job you would like to have and use that for your illustration.) Write down the job title, purpose, and what you actually do during the day. List the tasks that you do in order of importance. Use the blank format that follows to help you complete this exercise.

POSITION WRITE-UP

POSITION TITLE: DATE:

DEPARTMENT:

ACCOUNTABLE TO:

PRIMARY OBJECTIVE OF POSITION:

MAJOR AREAS OF ACCOUNTABILITY:

OTHER JOB REQUIREMENTS:

PREPARED BY: REVIEWED BY: APPROVED BY:

STAFFING

Once you discover you cannot do all of the work in the department yourself, you begin to feel you need *help*. That help comes in the form of people. At this point, you may start to panic, break into a cold sweat, and your palms may become sticky. Just relax. Take a deep breath, and let it out slowly. There really isn't a reason to panic, especially if you *know* what type of individual it is you want.

With a job description in your hand, you have a base from which you can start your search. If you post the job within the company, your personnel department can help you. However, if you do not have a personnel department, simply place the job description on a bulletin board with a note asking interested people to come and see you. When you need to go outside the company, place an ad in your local newspaper. The newspaper may be able to help you with the wording, but you may want to practice writing the ad yourself. What will your ad say? Start with the company name, address, and the job title. Include a summary of the job and any company benefits.

Once you have placed the ad, you need to know what you can or cannot ask the applicants. However, screening possible employees is a very easy process.

Remember, when you are armed with a job description and you know what you want — go for it!

Focus on Job-Related Abilities and Skills ONLY!

The questions you should ask should apply specifically to the job. Focus your attention only on job-related abilities and skills. Ask all applicants the *same questions* in the *same setting*. Your objective in the hiring process is to find the best possible person.

The following example is a list of questions which can be used in a job interview for filling a Quality Control Inspector position. Match these questions to the job description presented earlier and think about the related skills and abilities needed for the job.

Sample Text of an Interview

I will be asking you a series of questions during this interview about the quality control position you applied for. You will be able to ask me questions as we go along and also at the end of the interview.

Try to relax.

1. So that I can have a better or total picture of you, tell me some things about your background. (When the person states personal items, direct their comments to the job abilities and skills.)
2. What do you want from this job?
3. What do you believe makes you qualified for this position?
4. In your opinion, what is quality control?
5. What do you think the people in quality control do daily?
6. What are your hobbies?
7. Do you like to read? What do you like to read?
8. How would you judge your handwriting? Fair, Good, Excellent, Other: _____
9. Do you have plans for the future? What are they?
10. Do you have experience in using measuring tools? With which measuring tools?
11. How would you rate your print-reading skills? Fair, Good, Excellent
12. What do you like about your present job?
13. What do you dislike about your present job?
14. What did you like about your past jobs?
15. What did you dislike about your past jobs?
16. How would you handle this situation: A friend of yours has just manufactured some defective parts. What would you say to that person? What would you do?

I have asked you a number of questions. Do you have any questions for me?

Thank you for interviewing for this position. As soon as a decision is made, you will be informed of the selection.

(Shake hands with every applicant, regardless of their sex.)

In making your decision, rank all candidates making number one your first choice and so on down the list. Once the candidate is selected, contact all of the other candidates with your decision.

Do Not Ask — It is Not Your Business

Remember, do not ask questions that are not job related. Some questions *not* to ask are:

1. Age - date of birth
2. Citizenship
3. Family situation; i.e., number of children, ages of children, child-care provisions, etc.
4. Marital status
5. Credit or garnishment record
6. Public assistance status
7. Disabilities
8. Political or religious affiliations
9. Sexual preference

Your words or actions *must not* convey an incorrect or a biased impression.

Stay away from using words like: *gals, girls, boys, minorities, handicapped*. Do not use expressions which could be construed as flirting, patronizing, talking down to the person, etc.

A general rule of thumb in interviewing is to avoid asking questions that do not apply to the specific job or performance. Those personal questions are none of your business.

CONDUCTING AN INTERVIEW EXERCISE

LEADER:

Have the students pair off. Using the job descriptions that they prepared in the previous exercise, and the criteria on preparing for and conducting an interview, have each student role play conducting an interview with the other person in the group. After 15 minutes, have the students reverse roles and repeat the exercise. Work space is provided on page 101.

By having the students conduct interviews using the job descriptions that they prepared previously, each student will be intimately familiar with the position. This should strengthen the students' interviewing confidence and technique.

Directions: As a review, prepare and conduct an interview by using the following outline:

1. Define the major job duties.
2. Define the necessary knowledge, skills, and abilities needed to do the job. (These are part of the job description.)
3. List other job-related factors to consider, i.e., hours of work, travel, and overtime.
4. Develop questions to learn about necessary abilities and job-related factors.
5. Create a comfortable interviewing environment that is both quiet and private.
6. Conduct the interview.
    a. Describe the position accurately.
    b. *Ask job-related questions only.*
    c. Record the major points of the individuals answers.
    d. Ask the applicant if he or she has any questions.

If you were going to interview more than one individual, you would repeat steps 1-6 with each interviewee and then:

7. Rate the applicants.
8. Make your selection.
9. Contact the applicant you selected as your first choice.
10. Contact the applicants who were not selected.

LEADER:
Once this part of the exercise is completed, have the class discuss what they learned in doing the exercise and answer the following questions:
1. *Did the person use the information on how to prepare and conduct an interview?*
2. *Did the person being interviewed volunteer information that was not job related?*
3. *What did the interviewer say when the volunteered information was stated?*
4. *Would you hire the person you interviewed? Why or why not?*
5. *How could the person being interviewed improve and how could the person doing the interviewing improve?*

Performance Reviews

You have selected a person to work in your department and a period of time has passed. Now you need to give a performance review of that person's work.

There are three areas you need to focus on when a performance review is to be given. These areas are: the *Preinterview*, the *Interview*, and the *Post Interview*.

Preinterview

Planning is the focus of your efforts in this portion of the reviewing cycle. Your planning should include discussion of the following:

1. Achievements made by the individual during the reviewing period.
2. Recognition of his achievements during the reviewing period.
3. Responsibility for the tasks that have been given during the performance period.
4. Whether the individual's work is acceptable or not.
5. Advancement planning and consideration for advancement.
6. The individual's interpersonal relationship skills.

Use the job description. If possible, during the performance review period, write down positive and negative comments in a notebook to be used for your reference. The employee should be aware of this notebook and, if you use this approach, use it for *all* your employees.

When a negative situation occurs, discuss it at *that* time with the employee. Do not wait until the performance review. It can be brought up at the review and the action taken can be discussed.

Also, before you give a review, tell the employee when that review is scheduled. The individual should also be able to prepare for the review.

Interview

Now the focus is on the performance interview. Begin the discussion with the person in a friendly manner. Create an open atmosphere for discussing the positive and negative elements. Use this time to reinforce the positives with the employee for the total performance period. Remember the review is for the *total performance period*, not for one day's occurrence.

Discuss the job description. Follow this discussion with the job duties of the individual. Review the job duties and reinforce the positives. Discuss the negatives with the person and listen to the employee. Allow time to resolve problems, if possible. If there is a need, schedule a time to meet again. Close the interview by reinforcing the positives.

Post Interview

The third area to focus your attention on at this time is the post interview. During the post interview, discuss any decided-upon action with the employee — such as a salary adjustment, if needed. Then evaluate the effectiveness and method of your interview and make changes that would improve your skills.

PERFORMANCE REVIEW EXERCISE

Complete the performance review by circling the letter that best answers each question.

LEADER:
  a) Once each person has completed the individual part of this exercise, break into small groups and discuss the answers.
  b) In the groups, decide on one answer for each of the questions. Use the skills gained, i.e., leadership, problem solving, decision making, communicating and interviewing.
  c) Have one member from each group present to the class what his group discussed and report those activities to the total group.

1. For planning a performance appraisal you should:
   A. Pick out recent incidents or examples to help you evaluate the person's current performance level.
   B. Expand your review to cover the entire period since the last appraisal.
   C. Do nothing.
2. The top priority item in your planning should be:
   A. Review the employee's list of goals and objectives.
   B. Review the job description.
   C. Interview other supervisors and managers with whom the employee comes in contact.
3. Your main objective for this performance appraisal should be:
   A. Let the employee know where he stands.
   B. Solicit ideas and viewpoints, and improve your relationship.
   C. Upgrade the performance of the employee.
4. In preparing for the performance appraisal, you should:
   A. Plan to cover all of the strengths and weaknesses in detail to provide a comprehensive picture of the employee's work history.
   B. Concentrate only on weak areas.
   C. Plan to discuss the *key* strengths and weaknesses.
5. During the performance appraisal, the employee unexpectedly brings up the question of a raise. What is the best way of handling the situation?
   A. Explain you will recommend a salary increase if he can upgrade his performance in certain areas.
   B. Explain that the purpose of this appraisal is to discuss performance, and while compensation is related, you would like to defer money matters until a later, more appropriate time.
   C. Advise the person of the progress to date, and that you will discuss money matters at the end of the appraisal process.
6. The fact the employee has a problem has been agreed upon. How will you motivate the person to change?
   A. Tell the person what you want him to do and convince him.
   B. Use a nondirective approach to help the person develop a solution.
   C. Let the person correct the fault.
7. One approach to upgrade a person's performance would be a self-development plan. When you suggest the plan, the person enthusiastically agrees and says, "Let me see what I can come up with in the next week." What should you do?
   A. Allow the person to proceed as he suggested.
   B. Compliment the person on his enthusiasm, but suggest the plan should be *now*.
   C. Draft the plan yourself, with no input from your employee.
8. Your role in getting your employees to reach goals and objectives should be:
   A. Nonparticipative.
   B. Neutral.
   C. Participative.
9. You and your employee have completed the details of the development plan. In order to make sure the employee understands his role and for you to gauge the commitment, you should ask some questions. The *best* questions to ask at this time are:
   A. How does this plan sound to you?
   B. What do you feel will be the *most* difficult part of the plan to implement?
   C. "Are you with me so far?"
   D. All of the above.

ROLE PLAYING PERFORMANCE REVIEW EXERCISE

LEADER:

Another good practice exercise to complete is to role play a performance review. Have the class break into groups of two people. The first person has 10 minutes to give a performance review; this is followed by the other person giving a 10 minute review. Once the review is completed, discuss the problems each person had in completing this exercise, and the criteria that would have made the review more rewarding. In one large group, discuss what each individual group accomplished.

Directions: To gain practice, role play conducting a performance review. As the interviewer, you should be using the interviewee's job description as the basis for your evaluation. Use the performance review and performance rating forms provided to complete this exercise.

SALARIED PERFORMANCE REVIEW FORM

Review Date: _____

NAME: _____ REPORTS TO: _____

POSITION TITLE: _____

DEPARTMENT NAME AND NUMBER: _____

A. GOAL PERFORMANCE/ NOTABLE ACHIEVEMENTS/ SPECIAL PROBLEMS

_____

_____

_____

_____

_____

_____

_____

_____

COMMENT ON EMPLOYEE'S ATTENDANCE RECORD DURING THIS REVIEWING PERIOD:

_____

B. MAJOR AREAS OF ACCOUNTABILITY BASED ON JOB DESCRIPTION DATED: _____

Major Areas of Accountability Where Performance Was Clearly Above Standard.

Accountability Number	**Accountability Area**	**Comments**
_____ /	_____ /	_____
_____ /	_____ /	_____
_____ /	_____ /	_____

Major Areas of Accountability Where Performance Was Below Standard.

Accountability Number	Accountability Area	Comments
_____ /	_____ /	_____
_____ /	_____ /	_____
_____ /	_____ /	_____

C. CHARACTERISTICS THAT ADD TO OR DETRACT FROM OVERALL PERFORMANCE:
_____
_____

D. SIGNIFICANT CHANGES IN PERFORMANCE SINCE THE LAST REVIEW:
_____
_____

E. PLANS TO IMPROVE PERFORMANCE:
_____
_____

F. WHAT EDUCATION, TRAINING OR EXPERIENCE WOULD BENEFIT THE EMPLOYEE?
_____
_____

G. THE POSITION WRITE-UP FOR THIS EMPLOYEE _____ IS CURRENT
_____ NEEDS REVISION

H. SUMMARY EVALUATION OF OVERALL PERFORMANCE

/ _____ / _____ / _____ / _____ / _____ /

| Performance is Unacceptable | Performance Less Than Expected | Satisfactory Progress Expectations | Performance is Exceeding Expectations | Performance Far Exceeds Expectations |

I. COMMENTS ON REVIEW FROM THE EMPLOYEE:
_____
_____
_____

THIS REVIEW WAS EXAMINED BY _____ AND _____
(EMPLOYEE'S SIGNATURE)   (REVIEWER'S SIGNATURE)

DATE OF THE REVIEW _____

REVIEWED BY THE DEPARTMENT HEAD ON _____ SIGNATURE _____

NONEXEMPT PERFORMANCE REVIEW FORM

Review Date: _____

NAME _____ POSITION TITLE _____

DEPARTMENT _____ ACCOUNTABLE TO _____

A. MAJOR AREAS OF ACCOUNTABILITY ON POSITION WRITE-UP DATED: _____

    −   0   +   (KEY: − **Needs to Improve** ⁰ **Meets Requirements** ⁺ **Excellent**)

1. _____/_____/_____/ _____
   _____

2. _____/_____/_____/ _____
   _____

3. _____/_____/_____/ _____
   _____

4. _____/_____/_____/ _____
   _____

5. _____/_____/_____/ _____
   _____

6. _____/_____/_____/ _____
   _____

B. CHARACTERISTICS THAT ADD TO OR DETRACT FROM OVERALL PERFORMANCE.
   _____
   _____

C. KEY AREAS WHERE PERFORMANCE HAS BEEN EXCELLENT OR CAN BE IMPROVED.
   _____
   _____
   _____

D. WHAT EDUCATION, TRAINING OR EXPERIENCE WOULD BENEFIT THIS EMPLOYEE?
   _____
   _____

E. WAS THE POSITION WRITE-UP REVIEWED DURING THE CONFERENCE? _____

F. POSITION WRITE-UP _____ IS CURRENT
                        _____ NEEDS REVISION

G. SUMMARY OF OVERALL PERFORMANCE

/ _____ / _____ / _____ / _____ / _____ /

| **Performance Below Desired Level** | **Making Progress** | **Meets All Requirements** | **Exceeds Performance Requirements** | **Superior** |

H. COMMENTS ON REVIEW BY THE EMPLOYEE.
   _____
   _____
   _____

THIS FORM WAS REVIEWED BY _____ AND _____
(EMPLOYEE'S SIGNATURE) (REVIEWER'S SIGNATURE)
DATE OF THE REVIEW _____
REVIEWED AND APPROVED BY _____ DATE _____

EMPLOYEE PERFORMANCE RATING

NAME _____ JOB TITLE _____
DEPARTMENT _____ RESPONSIBILITY LEVEL _____

Evaluate the employee's performance with respect to quantity and quality of work. Rate the employee's personal characteristics by circling the most appropriate number, using the descriptive comments as guides.

1. JOB KNOWLEDGE   1   2   3   4   5   6   7   8   9   10
   /_____/_____/_____/_____/_____/
   POOR   MARGINAL   MEETS   SUPERIOR   OUTSTANDING
   PERFORMER   JOB
                                     REQUIREMENTS

2. DEPENDABILITY   1   2   3   4   5   6   7   8   9   10
   /_____/_____/_____/_____/_____/
   ABSENT   OCCASIONALLY GOOD   RARELY LATE   NEVER LATE
   OFTEN   LATE   OR ABSENT   OR ABSENT

3. COOPERATION   1   2   3   4   5   6   7   8   9   10
   /_____/_____/_____/_____/_____/
   SURLY OR   OCCASIONALLY COURTEOUS   ALWAYS   ALWAYS VERY
   UNFRIENDLY   UNWILLING   COURTEOUS   COURTEOUS
                     TO FOLLOW
                     INSTRUCTIONS

4. INITIATIVE   1   2   3   4   5   6   7   8   9   10
   /_____/_____/_____/_____/_____/
   NO DESIRE   LEARNS   ABLE TO   LEARNS NEW   LIKES TO
                     SLOWLY   LEARN   TASKS WITH-   MASTER NEW
                                                     OUT PROBLEM   SKILLS

5. COMMENTS _____
   _____

6. OVERALL EVALUATION
   /_____/_____/_____/
   LOW QUANTITY AND   MEETS AND MAINTAINS   ABOVE ESTABLISHED
   QUALITY   ESTABLISHED STANDARDS   STANDARDS

7. THIS APPRAISAL COVERS PERFORMANCE FOR THE _____ PREVIOUS MONTHS PERIOD.
8. EMPLOYEE'S COMMENTS _____
   _____
   _____

9. PERFORMANCE EVALUATION MADE BY _____ DATE _____
   REVIEWED AND APPROVED BY _____ DATE _____
   WITH THE DISCUSSION OF _____ ON _____.
         (EMPLOYEE'S SIGNATURE)   DATE

DELEGATION

DELEGATION

Delegation. "Who me?"
"Why not?"
Why do managers hesitate to use delegation as a management tool?

— Fear their employees will outperform them.
— Fear of exposing weaknesses in their own competence to get the job completed.
— A belief the work will not be done properly unless they do it themselves.
— They may enjoy doing the task and are reluctant to let someone else do it — in other words *control*.
— They may not understand their management jobs.
— Fear of what their employees and peers think of them for not doing the job.

Can you think of other reasons managers and supervisors do not delegate jobs? (The list may include resistance by employees in accepting more responsibilities, resistance by employees to learn new tasks, etc.)

Steps of Delegation

Some managers delegate responsibility in steps, especially with employees who have never performed a particular task or who have never experienced delegated responsibility. There are different steps of delegation, ranging from a simple fact-finding mission to actually making the final decision — or, as some would say, "Doing the mission impossible."

Delegation can be used as both a training tool for the employee and information for you, as the manager.

There are several approaches to delegation. The first step is to have the employee do the actual investigation, let's say, of a problem. He or she then brings all of the facts to the manager. The manager makes the final decision and takes any other action that is necessary. The next step would be for the employee to both do the investigation and make decision recommendations on handling the problem. At this point, the manager makes the final decision and takes the necessary action. Another approach in delegating responsibilities is to simply give the employee full responsibility for the task or project you have in mind, and have him proceed on his own.

You can certainly use the different steps of delegation to get your employees into the delegation process. However, whichever method you use, be sure the employees who have been given the opportunity for the challenges of delegation have been trained. Their skills and abilities are a factor in delegating responsibilities.

"How do I go about delegating?" That is a very good question. Delegation depends on the working relationship between the manager, supervisor, and each employee in the department as well as on each employee's ability and interest. These are of primary importance when you want the delegation process to work effectively. There are some general guidelines to follow to assure your delegation efforts are successful:

— Delegate what is wanted and needed by you, your manager, and the organization.
— Delegate with the results you have in mind.
— Set performance standards and guidelines that can be measured.
— Give the employee all of the information needed so he can complete the job.
— Delegate to competent employees.
— Delegate to employees whom you wish to train.
— Delegate to employees to determine their competency level.

Authority and Responsibility

The authority and responsibility to delegate needs to be passed down from the highest level in the organization to the lowest level of the organization. Of course, this applies only to the lowest organization level that has the competence and knowledge to complete the job.

You can use the technique of delegation to train and increase the ability of employees who might be having job- or task-related problems.

As a manager, you cannot abdicate your leadership responsibility to others in your department. You can delegate without fear as long as *you* are in charge of your department. Managers and employees alike need to understand that authority and responsibility can be delegated, but not *accountability*. The manager is the person ultimately accountable for any problems in his department.

What can you delegate?

That is a good question.

In order to answer this, we need to break the question into three sections. First, we deal with the work the manager can presently complete; this is followed by deciding which work can be delegated to qualified employees; then deciding which tasks can be delegated immediately. More specifically, the work the manager can complete includes his role duties as department leader. This also covers those tasks the manager cannot delegate, and those routine jobs he may delegate.

When can an employee take on the task of delegation?

First, the manager needs to identify which work can be delegated. Secondly, the manager must identify the special training and development needed by the employee. Thirdly, if the manager determines the employee is ready, the task of delegation can take place.

Delegation: Now!

When the manager determines the employee is ready for delegated responsibilities, the next step is . . . delegation. But just a minute, have you, as manager, considered the following items?

1. Is the employee able to do the work or task?
2. Is the employee interested in doing the work and doing it well?
3. Has the employee completed this type of work in the past, what were the results, and does it make a difference?

Benefits of Delegation

In more than one circle of management thought exists the belief that when an employee is involved in the decision-making process, there is a direct relationship between his increased productivity and job satisfaction. How can you, as the manager, involve the employee? Through delegation!

Increased self-respect is one positive effect of delegation felt by the employee. When you give an individual a task to perform — and let him make his own decisions — he has a personal interest in the results produced. Delegation also gives the manager and employee confidence in one another's abilities to get the job completed. The confidence of the organization in you, as an employee, is increased.

An employee who works for a delegating manager has an excellent opportunity to learn. One of the best preparations for a position requiring decision-making skills is to have been given full responsibility for delegated tasks.

The manager also receives benefits from the delegation process. The most obvious is the freedom to do other tasks. Receiving more time for planning the present and future department goals is another benefit for the manager. Other benefits include developing new and better job techniques and establishing better working relationships with peers and superiors.

What other benefits would there be for you, as the manager, and your employees when you are willing to delegate tasks?

CASE STUDY: DO YOU DELEGATE?

This exercise is designed to help you determine how and what you can delegate to your department employees.

LEADER:
Before dividing the class into small work groups, help the students come up with a list of

routine tasks. Do not discuss possible delegation at this point. Have each group use the task list to complete the exercise.

Directions: Read the exercise and complete the questions. Be prepared to discuss your answers in small groups.

You are a department manager. You have five employees who report directly to you. Each employee has individual strengths and weaknesses, and you want to broaden the scope of their jobs. You also want to turn their weaknesses into strengths. It seems that you are stuck doing routine tasks. You want to delegate some of those tasks, as well as special projects, to employees in the department.

The five employees in the department are described as follows:

1. Allen:
He has been in your department for three years. His total length of time with the organization has been over ten years. He tends to be busy, but you are concerned that his time is not spent wisely.

2. Karen:
She is a very assertive person. She has been with the organization for fifteen years and has been in your department for five years. Karen has experience in many different departments, but she does not seem to have enough time to do routine job tasks. She is more than willing to take on special projects.

3. Jeff:
He has been with your department two years, ever since he first started work for the organization. Jeff seems to be immature at times; he has some problems working in groups, especially as the leader. He is an average worker, and he gets the job done.

4. Steve:
Steve is retiring next year. He is an assertive person and easily handles problems in groups. He knows how to problem-solve when working alone. He is well liked and an above-average performer. He likes project work, too.

5. Shara:
She has been in the United States for one year and has been in your department for six months. Shara has a Masters Degree in Business Management. She is a very good employee and a hard worker. However, while working in groups, employees have sometimes complained they do not understand her. She is assertive and enjoys solving problems.

Your task is to provide ways and plans for your employees to become better workers. You also need to delegate. Work through the following questions:

1. What tasks could you delegate to your employees? List them.
2. Do you delegate tasks to *each* employee and to whom do you delegate which tasks and why? (Use your list.) If you choose *not* to delegate work to any employee, explain why not.
3. Do some employees need to be trained before giving them any responsibilities? If so, who and what type of training would you give them?
4. Do you trust each employee with the delegated responsibilities? How do you show the employees you trust them?
5. How do you build confidence in your employees to handle emergencies on their own?
6. How are the employees going to communicate with you during special projects and long-term delegation responsibilities?
7. If your employees make incorrect decisions, how are you going to help them figure out what went wrong? How do you make the corrections — or do *you*?

BUDGETING

BUDGETING

Budgets are a control device. They are developed from established standards where operations are compared, appraised, and adjusted. Budgets also provide information which guides the supervisor and manager in taking action and conforming to a plan.

A typical budget has the following information to help you as the manager:

1. Department numbers
2. Account numbers
3. Account titles
4. A plan with dollar amounts
5. Actual dollars active in each account
6. Variance percent comparing year-to-year or month-to-month
7. Comparison between accounts planned and actual month-to-month use
8. Comparison between percentage of the total budget plan and its actual use

As a management tool, the budget can be used to help determine which accounts can be kept active and which accounts can be cut.

Accounts that may be considered in a manufacturing setting include labor (direct and indirect), maintenance and repair charges, utilities, operating supplies, rework, scrap, and returns.

Does all of this sound confusing?

A good comparison to a business budget would be a budget used at home. Your home budget may have some of the same account names the business budget uses: utilities, maintenance, repair, operating supplies. When maintained efficiently, both home and business budgets are good, sound management techniques for control.

BUDGETING EXERCISE

Directions: For an exercise, you are going to develop a home budget. If you do not have one, apply the business skills of management in developing your home budget. Your accounts are to include: income, insurance, food, clothes, rent (mortgage payment), utilities, phone, and transportation. You may want to add more accounts to your budget.

Work out the budget using *projected* income and expenses for *one month*, *one quarter*, and *one year*. Keep a running total of *actual* income and expenses for each month, so you know where you are.

A sample budget is provided for you. This budget can be used to help you develop further exercises.

ACCOUNT NUMBER	DESCRIPTION	F84	F85	F86
020	Salaries and Wages	144,000	112,000	161,000
030	Overtime	600	50	0
035	Temporary Help	200	30	0
040	Sick Pay	15	5	0
050	Holiday Pay	3,500	3,500	4,000
055	Vacation Pay	9,000	5,000	4,000
090	Worker's Comp. Insurance	3,000	7,000	9,000
095	Hiring Expense	500	0	0
120	Shop Supplies	2,000	1,000	1,000
130	Tool Expense	3,000	2,300	3,000
135	Office Supplies	6,000	5,000	3,500
137	Equipment Repair	600	400	1,000
140	Professional Services	600	0	600
150	Lodging	70	0	200
155	Meals	15	4	100
160	Transportation	700	1,490	1,500
200	Education	500	1,000	1,500
210	Dues and Subscriptions	300	300	500
300	Telephone	1,100	1,500	2,000
	Department Totals	175,700	149,575	192,900

Benefits of Budgets

What are the benefits of a budget? These benefits could be applied to your home budget as well as your business budget:

1. Defines home, department, and company objectives and policies.
2. Weighs business and home strategies.
3. Is a tool to help you and management make better decisions.
4. Provides a way to determine the effective uses of capital equipment and resources.
5. Provides a way to determine the effective use of family and employee resources.
6. Improves coordination and communication with management, family, and employees.
7. Guards against waste.
8. Is a warning system for early detection of negative and positive changes.

There are many factors in determining the appropriate budget for your organization or home.

Because of individual needs and wants, no single budgeting system would be appropriate for every company or home. Some of the limiting factors may include resources, standards, size of the organization or family, or type of organization or family.

LABOR RELATIONS

LABOR RELATIONS

There are primarily two types of organizations in the United States: union and nonunion organizations.

Union Organizations

In union organizations, the first rule as a manager or supervisor is to *read the contract*. The contract provides information on:
1. The role of the supervisor and manager.
2. The role of the employee or union members.
3. The application of the contract, i.e., the interpretation, rights, difficulties, and handling of grievances.

You also need to know what the grievance procedure is. Different unions and companies have different procedures for handling a grievance, but generally, a typical procedure would include the following:
1. Appellate process.
2. Negotiation.
3. Arbitration (terminal step).

During a grievance meeting, the grievance needs to be discussed and reviewed. The skills used are very similar to the various communication and leadership skills discussed in previous chapters of this book, including:

- Not becoming angry — listening.
- Defining the real problem and working on it.
- Getting all of the facts.
- Checking the contract.
- Considering the consequences of this settlement compared to past settlements.
- Being consistent.
- Giving clear answers and asking for clarification where needed.
- Keeping accurate records.

When there is a discipline problem, use the system in the contract. That system may suggest:
1. Verbal warning for the first violation.
2. Written warning for the second violation.
3. Suspension for the third violation.
4. Termination as the last step.

Most of the problems will end at the grievance level. However, when an agreement or consensus cannot be reached during the grievance process, arbitration is the next step. Arbitration is formal settlement of a dispute. The union and the company, by process of elimination, agree on the selection of an arbitrator, who presides over the hearing as a judge would preside over a court trial. Although held out of court, an arbitration is run very much like a trial and the parties involved are bound to abide by the decision of the arbitrator, as they would be the judge in a court of law.

The legal departments representing the union and the company brief their respective sides, and a preliminary conference is held. Witnesses are contacted and evidence is preserved.

The hearing begins. A special preparation of contract interpretation is presented. Witnesses, while under oath, testify and may be cross-examined. Evidence is presented. At the conclusion, the arbitrator makes the ultimate decision as to the outcome of the dispute based on the evidence and testimony that has been presented. The arbitrator is paid for his or her services, and the matter is considered to be concluded.

Nonunion Organizations

For nonunion organizations, the process is much the same with the exception of two points: state laws and a union arbitration.

State laws would govern the rights of employees and employers in a point of dispute. Each state has many ways of dealing with human rights. It is suggested that supervisors and managers know the laws of their state. In most cases, the personnel department of an organization would have that information.

In case your organization is without a personnel department — what *can* you do?

You may need to establish:
1. Sound employee policies which are written for the whole organization, not for just one department.
2. A grievance procedure which would include some of the same items a union organization might. Again, this should be an organization-wide plan, not just a departmental plan. The procedure may include:
   a. Being available to your employees.
   b. Listening to your employees.
   c. Not becoming angry — listening.
   d. Defining the real problem.
   e. Getting all of the facts.
   f. Avoiding delays or communicating delays beyond your control to your employees.
   g. Being consistent.
   h. Giving clear answers and asking for clarification where needed.
   i. Keeping accurate records.
3. A discipline system. Generally, it would reflect a union organization system.

As a final thought about labor relations in an organization, keep these three suggestions in mind for building positive relationships between yourself (the supervisor) and your employees:
- Be fair.
- Be honest.
- Be consistent.

REASSESSMENT

REASSESSMENT

We have taken a look at skills that every supervisor should possess or attain. Briefly, the skills include familiarity and knowledge of the work force, leadership, communication, decision making, problem solving, employee motivation, time management and planning, organization, staffing, delegation, budgeting, and labor relations.

At the beginning of this class, you took a brief assessment of your personal goals and supervisory skills. With the new knowledge and information you have attained by reading this text and participating and sharing in group discussions, perhaps your views have changed somewhat. It is time to reassess yourself.

You will end this class much as you began it, by once again completing the self-examination exercise below.

SELF-EXAMINATION EXERCISE

You are to analyze yourself by thoughtfully and honestly answering the ten category questions. In answering each question in each category, grade yourself by using the following scale:

> 4 . . . . . . Superior
> 3 . . . . . . Above Average
> 2 . . . . . . Average
> 1 . . . . . . Below Average

Once you have graded each question, place your total in the space provided in the "Your Present Strengths Summary" at the end of this exercise.

The results are for your confidential use, so please be direct and honest with yourself.

1. Aspiration
   _____ A. Can you describe your life goal in logical terms?
   _____ B. Does your goal challenge the very utmost of your ability?
   _____ C. Have you worked out a plan for attaining your goal?
   _____ D. Are you ready to give up other aims and pleasures to be successful?

2. Knowledge
   _____ A. How does your present knowledge compare with knowledge that is possible to gain?
   _____ B. Do you faithfully follow the rule of gaining knowledge when needed?
   _____ C. How much pride do you take in learning something new daily?
   _____ D. To what extent are you open to new knowledge, ideas, and methods?

3. Ambition
   _____ A. When you see something that should be done, do you consistently start right out to do it?
   _____ B. Are you willing to work before or after hours to develop new ideas connected with your job?
   _____ C. Are you willing to share your ideas with others?
   _____ D. Is your initiative backed up by determination to finish what you start?

4. Thoroughness
   _____ A. Do your efforts go beyond what you have been asked to do?
   _____ B. Do you perform disagreeable tasks?
   _____ C. When you have something to do, do you search for the very best way of accomplishing it?
   _____ D. Do you refuse to pass judgment on any matter until all the facts have been weighed?

5. Investigative Powers
   _____ A. Do you frequently see ways of making practical use of information that comes to you daily?
   _____ B. Do you think something through to form your own opinions rather than accepting the opinions of others?

_____ C. Do you "dig down" to get at the bottom of problems?
_____ D. When you have all the facts, how successful are you in rejecting personal prejudice and other people's biased opinions?

6. Decision Making

_____ A. How much satisfaction do you find in your responsibility for important decisions?
_____ B. To what extent are your decisions based on well thought-out reasons?
_____ C. Do you procrastinate in making final decisions on important questions?
_____ D. When you have made a decision, how confidently do you put it into effect?

7. Leadership

_____ A. How much confidence do you have when you know you are right?
_____ B. Are you considerate of the rights and feelings of others?
_____ C. Do you retain the good will of your associates when you have to criticize them?
_____ D. Do you believe your associates listen to your views or concepts with confidence and respect?
_____ E. Do you inspire confidence in others?
_____ F. Do you meet criticism without losing your temper?

8. Organizing Ability

_____ A. Do you analyze the problems that confront you?
_____ B. Are you successful in separating tasks into smaller ones your employees can more easily complete?
_____ C. Do you follow a systematic plan in assigning and doing tasks?

9. Problem Solving

_____ A. Do you develop new ideas to use in solving problems?
_____ B. When things are going wrong do you suggest ways for improving them?
_____ C. Do you study what you do with the intent of finding a better way to complete it?
_____ D. Do your employees and peers consider your ideas practical?

10. Application

_____ A. Do you analyze your successes or failures?
_____ B. Do you analyze the success or failure of others?
_____ C. Are you the first person to suggest a practical solution to a problem?
_____ D. Do you learn the principles that apply to work other than your own for a total view?

Your Present Strengths Summary

_____ 1. Aspiration
_____ 2. Knowledge
_____ 3. Ambition
_____ 4. Thoroughness
_____ 5. Investigative Powers
_____ 6. Decision Making
_____ 7. Leadership
_____ 8. Organizing Ability
_____ 9. Problem Solving
_____ 10. Application

Compare your second set of answers with your previous answers from when you completed the test for the first time. Perhaps you will be pleasantly surprised to discover that you gained — rather painlessly — some new strengths over the course of time it took to get from cover to cover of *So You Are the Supervisor*.

Good luck in your supervisory role, and may it be a stepping stone for things to come.

BIBLIOGRAPHY

BIBLIOGRAPHY

LEADERSHIP

Books

Albanese, Robert. *Management: Toward Accountability for Performance.* Homewood, Ill.: Richard D. Irwin, 1975.

Bass, Bernard M. and James A. Vaughan. *The Management of Learning.* Belmont, Calif.: Brooks, Cole Pub., 1966.

Bittel, Lester R. *What Every Supervisor Should Know.* New York: McGraw-Hill, 1974.

Blanchard, Kenneth and Spencer Johnson. *The One-Minute Manager.* New York: Berkley Pub., 1982.

Byrd, Richard E. *A Guide To Personal Risk Taking.* New York: AMACOM, 1974.

Drucker, Peter F. *Effective Executive.* New York: Harper & Row, 1967.

Drucker. *Management: Tasks, Responsibilities, Practices.* New York: Harper & Row, 1974.

Drucker. *Managing for Results.* New York: Harper & Row, 1964.

Drucker. *Practice of Management.* New York: Harper & Row, 1954.

Fridler, Fred E. and Martin M. Chemers. *Leadership and Effective Management.* Glenview, Ill.: Scott, Foresman & Co., 1974.

Golightly, Henry O. *Managing with Style.* New York: AMACOM, 1977.

Grossman, Lee. *The Change Agent.* New York: AMACOM, 1974.

Harris, Thomas A. *I'm OK-You're OK.* New York: Avon, 1973.

Knowles, Malcolm. *The Adult Learner: A Neglected Species.* Houston: Gulf Pub., 1973.

Monthly Publications

"Executive Action Series" (monthly publication). Waterford, Conn.: Bureau of Business Practice.

"Quality Control Supervisor's Bulletin" (semimonthly publication). Waterford, Conn.: Bureau of Business Practice.

Films

American Media, Inc. "Everything You Always Wanted To Know About Supervision." Color, 28 minutes, 1980. This is a story of a young woman who has become a supervisor. She learns how to plan, delegate, discipline, and communicate.

CRM/McGraw-Hill Films. "Managing Stress." Color, 34 minutes, 1979. Increase longevity — This film shows how.

American Media, Inc./Philips Office Associates, Inc. "That's Not in My Job Description." Color, 19 minutes, 1981. This film covers a broader range of harassment than other films. The film also demonstrates individuals taking action to fight harassment problems.

COMMUNICATIONS

Books

Burley-Allen, Madelyn. *Listening: The Forgotten Skill.* New York: John Wiley & Sons, 1982.

Burely-Allen. *Managing Assertively: How to Improve Your People Skills.* New York: John Wiley & Sons, 1983.

Gilbert, Marilyn. *Clear Writing: A Business Guide.* New York: John Wiley & Sons, 1983.

Lararus, Sy. *Loud and Clear: Guide to Effective Communications.* New York: AMACOM, 1975.

O'Rourke, Terrence J. *A Basic Course in Manual Communication.* Silver Spring, Md.: Nat. Assoc. of the Deaf, 1973.

Pickens, Judy E., Patricia Walsh, and Linda Cook-Roberts. *Without Bias: A Guidebook for Nondiscriminatory Communication.* San Francisco: Int'l Assoc. of Bus. Comm., 1977.

Staley, John D. *Effective Communication on the Job.* New York: AMACOM, 1981.

Films

CRM/McGraw-Hill Films. "The Case of the Snarled Parking Lot." Color, 22 minutes, 1981. Short, fast, and funny. This film shows real-life situations in a variety of ways. There are four traps that are clearly exposed in this case study.

AIMS Instructional Media Services, Inc. "Communications: The Company Grapevine." Color, 26 minutes, 1983. Dramatized case study. Bill Hillman has problems with his employees. He fails to see and understand the problems. The lack of accurate information causes Bill to lose credibility, trust, and confidence.

DECISION MAKING/PROBLEM SOLVING

Books

Boyer, Howard E., editor. *Failure Analysis and Prevention*, Vol. 10. Metal Park, Ohio: ASM, 1975.

Kepner, Charles H. and Benjamin B. Tregoe. *The Rational Manager.* New York: McGraw-Hill, 1965.

Kidwell, John L. *Closed-Loop Corrective Action System.* Dayton, Ohio: John L. Kidwell Co. [undated].

Ulschak, Francis L., Leslie Nathanson, and Peter G. Gillan. *Small Group Problem Solving: An Aid to Organization Effectiveness.* Reading, Mass.: Addison-Wesley, 1981.

Films

Callner Film Production, Barr Films. "Alternatives and Information." Color, 17 minutes, 1982. Examines the heart of decision making. The situation in this film involves Frank Webster who has been promoted to a supervisory position and is in a crisis situation because he doesn't know how to make decisions.

CRM Productions, CRM/McGraw-Hill Films. "Conflict on the Line: A Case Study." Color, 15 minutes, 1982. Conflict arises on the line between Dan and his supervisor, Shirley. A carefully designed freeze frame ending allows maximum creativity in the presentation.

International Cinemedia Ltd., Journal Films, Inc. "Decision Making." Color, 20 minutes, 1980. Ethical questions and obligations of the employee/employer relationship. Problems of employee theft, waste, reduction, and time loss are considered.

CRM/McGraw-Hill Films. "Creative Problem Solving — How to Get Better Ideas." Color, 28 minutes, 1979. Creative problem solving can be developed, but is often inhibited.

MOTIVATION

Books

Maslow, A.H. *Motivation and Personality.* New York: Harper & Row, 1954.

Dewar, Donald L. *Quality Circles Leader Manual and Instructional Guide.* Red Bluff, Calif.: Quality Circle Inst., 1980.

Dowling, William. *Effective Management and the Behavioral Sciences.* New York: AMACOM, 1978.

Fulmer, Robert M. *The New Management.* New York: Macmillan, 1974.

Films

Salenger Educational Media. "Almost Everything You Wanted to Know about Motivating People, or Maslow's Hierarchy of Needs." Color, 15 minutes, 1975. This film will acquaint the viewer with Maslow's theory regarding human motivation. The film explores human motivation as it applies to work situations.

BNA Communications Inc. "Building A Climate for Individual Growth." Color, 25 minutes, 1969. Herzberg recommends a psychological analysis of managers' real growth rather than looking for status symbols as measures of advancement.

CRM/McGraw-Hill films. "The Power of Positive Reinforcement." Color, 28 minutes, 1978. Behavior modification with emphasis on positive reinforcement is the focus of this film.

PLANNING

Books

Delberg, Andre L, Andrew H. Van de Ven, and David Gustafson. *Group Techniques for Program Planning.* Glenwood, Ill., Scott, Foresman & Co., 1975.

Ferner, Jack D. *Successful Time Management.* New York: John Wiley & Sons, 1980.

Juran, J.M. and Frank M. Gryna, Jr. *Quality Planning and Analysis.* New York: McGraw-Hill, 1970.

Mager, Robert F. *Goal Analysis.* Belmont, Calif.: Fearon Pub., 1972.

Films

BNA Communications, Inc. "Colt — A Case Study." Color, 27 minutes, 1969. This is a case study of an actual company, Colt Heating and Ventilation Ltd., and presents the process involved in lauching their MBO (Management By Objective) program.

CRM Productions, CRM/McGraw-Hill Films. "Finding Time." Color, 30 minutes, 1980. Discusses some of the reasons for time scheduling problems. A set of specific "how-to" suggestions gives pointers that can help any worker better manage time.

ORGANIZATION

Books

Brown, J. Douglas. *The Human Nature of Organizations.* New York: AMACOM, 1973.

Juran, J.M., editor. *Quality Control Handbook,* 3rd edition. New York: McGraw-Hill, 1974.

Kidwell, John L. *Quality Organization Guidelines.* Dayton, Ohio: John L. Kidwell Co. [undated].

Minor, Robert S. and Clark W. Fetridge. *Office Administration Handbook.* Chicago: Dartnell Corp., 1981.

Robert, Gen. Henry M. *Robert's Rules of Order.* Glenview, Ill., Scott, Foresman & Co., 1970.

Ulschak, Francis L., Leslie Nathanson, and Pete G. Gillan. *Small Group Problem Solving: An Aid to Organizational Effectiveness.* Reading, Mass.: Addison-Wesley, 1981.

Film

BNA Communications, Inc. "Confronting Conflict." Color, 30 minutes, 1971. Portrays a management group actively working at developing itself into a management team. Areas involved are: emotional expression on the job, leadership, and the role of women in management.

STAFFING

Books

Bolles, Richard Nelson. *What Color Is Your Parachute?* Berkeley, Calif.: Ten Speed Press, 1972.

Broadwell, Martin M. *Moving Up to Supervision.* New York: Van Nostrand Reinhold, 1979.

Deegan, Arthur X., II. *Coaching: A Management Skill for Improving Individual Performance.* Reading, Mass., Addison-Wesley, 1984.

Haimann, Theo and Raymond Hilgert. *Supervision Concepts and Practices of Management.* Cincinnati, Ohio: South-Western Pub., 1977.

Mager, Robert F. and Peter Pipe. *Analyzing Performance Problems.* Belmont, Calif.: Fearon Pub., 1970.

Pleninger, Andrew. *How to Survive and Market Yourself in Management.* New York: AMACOM, 1977.

Roseman, Edward. *Confronting Nonpromotability.* New York: AMACOM, 1977.

Weiss, W.H. *Supervisor's Standard Reference Handbook.* Englewood Cliffs, N.J.: Prentice-Hall, 1982.

Films

Bureau of Business Practice. "How Supervisors Should Appraise Employee Performance." Color, 23 minutes, 1979. Shows supervisors how to conduct appraisals to reduce turnover.

Sandler Institutional Films, Inc./Barr Films. "The Interview Film." Color, 21 minutes, 1977. The interviewer sifts through the strengths and weaknesses of five applicants. Inside look at the procedures from an employer's point of view.

DELEGATION

Books

Haimann, Theo and Raymond L. Hilgert. *Supervision: Concepts and Practices of Management.* Cincinnati, Ohio: South-Western Pub., 1977.

McConkey, Dale D. *No-Nonsense Delegation.* New York: AMACOM, 1974.

Steinmetz, Lawrence L. *The Art and Skill of Delegation.* Reading, Mass.: Addison-Wesley, 1976.

Films

Trilcon Productions. "Delegation." VCR (¾ "), color, 7 minutes, 1983. Dramatizes six steps to be followed for successful delegation, explaining why, terms of results, authority, deadline, feedback, and control.

CRM Productions, CRM/McGraw-Hill films. "A Case of Working Smarter, Not Harder." Color, 7 minutes, 1983. This case study provides a practical role model. A how-to lesson for supervisors and managers who are uncertain about how to delegate and clears up the differences between delegating and "dumping." A comprehensive leaders guide is available with the film.

Walt Disney Productions. "Cost." Color, 20 minutes, 1977. Example of keeping track of costs.

LABOR RELATIONS

Books

Bittel, Lester R. *What Every Supervisor Should Know.* New York: McGraw-Hill, 1974.

Reynolds, Lloyd G. *Labor Economics and Labor Relations.* Englewood Cliffs, N.J.: Prentice-Hall, 1974.

Film

CRM/McGraw-Hill films. "Grievance." B & W, 30 minutes, 1954. This movie illustrates grievance and arbitration procedures.

INDEX

INDEX

A
Absenteeism, causes of, 17-18
Active listening, 41-42
Agenda, need for, in meetings, 31
Aggressive behavior, 62
Arbitration, 123
Assertive behavior, 62
Attitude, as element in motivation, 61

B
Behavior, as element in motivation, 62
Brainstorming, use of, in problem solving, 51
Budgeting, 117
   benefits of, 120
   exercise in, 118
   lesson plan for, 13

C
Check and balance area, of organizing, 89
Civil Rights Act of 1964, Title VII, 17
Communication, 37
   active listening, 41-43
   downward, 40
   as element in motivation, 60
   forms of, 41-43
   giving instructions and orders to employees, 43-44
   grapevine, 41
   lesson plan for, 9-10
   one-way, 37-39
   peer, 41
   two-way, 38-40
   upward, 40-41
   verbal, 41
   within an organization, 40-41
Constructive criticism, 68
Corrective action, 53
Course description, 3-4
Criticism, handling, 68

D
Decision making, 47
   case study, 53-54
   lesson plan for, 10
   obstacles in good, 47
   overcoming the obstacles in good, 47
   process of, 47

Delegation, 111
   authority and responsibility, 111-112
   benefits of, 112
   case study of, 112-113
   as element in motivation, 60-61
   lesson plan for, 13
   steps of, 111
   tasks for, 112
   timing of, 112
Discipline, handling, 65
Discipline problems, causes of, and corrective actions, 67-68
Downward communication, 40

E
Employees, giving instructions and orders to, 43-44
Employee turnover, case study of, 63
Equal Pay Amendment (1963) of the Fair Labor Standards Act of 1938, 17
"Espirit de corps," 62
Extrasensory perception, 42

F
Feedback, 40-41
Flat organization structure, 90
Foresmanship Foundation, 18
Formal communication, 41

G
Grapevine communication, 41
Grievance meeting, 123

H
Herzberg, Frederick, 59
Hierarchy of needs theory, 58-59

I
Informal communication, 41
Interview
   conducting, 100-101
   for performance reviews, 102
   sample questions for, 99-100
Introduction, lesson plan for, 7

J
Job descriptions. *See* Position write-ups.

L

Labor relations
  arbitration, 123
  grievance meetings, 123
  lesson plan for, 14
  nonunion organizations, 123-124
  union organizations, 123
Leadership, 27
  exercise on, 27-29
  lesson plan for, 8-9
  practicing skills of, 32-33
  qualities of, 29
  skills of, 30-32
  team or participative style, 29
Lesson plans
  budgeting, 13
  communication, 9-10
  decision making, 10
  delegation, 13
  introduction, 7
  labor relations, 14
  leadership, 8-9
  motivation, 11
  organizing/organization, 12-13
  planning, 11-12
  problem solving, 10
  time management, 11-12
  work force, 8
Listening, active, 41-42
Loop-closing period of organizing, 89

M

Management by objectives (MBO), 83-85
Manager
  exercise on ideal, 20-22
  functions of, 20
  qualities of good, 19-23
  self-examination exercise on, 22-23
Maslow, A. H., 58-59
Materials, 3
McGregor, Douglas, 59
Meetings, using leadership skills in, 30-31
Men, salary level of, 17
Morale, as element in motivation, 62-63

Motivation, 57
  behavioral science theory on, 58-59
  elements of, 60-63
  environment for, 60
  exercise in, 57-58
  lesson plan for, 11
  misconceptions about, 58

N

Negative action, 65
Negative attitude, changing, 61
Nonassertive behavior, 62

O

Observation, use of, in measuring morale, 63
Older workers, in the work force, 19
One-way communication, 37-39
Organizing/organization
  check and balance area, 89
  interviewing, 100-101
  lesson plan for, 12-13
  loop-closing period, 89
  organizational structures, 90-91
  performance reviews, 102-108
  planning period, 89
  position write-ups, 91-98
  staffing, 99-100

P

Participative leadership style, 29
Participative management, 60
Peer communication, 41
Performance reviews, 102
  exercise in, 102-108
  interview, 102
  post interview, 102
  preinterview, 102
  salaried review, 104-105
  sample form for nonexempt review, 106-108
Plan
  characteristics of good, 71
  example of five year quality, 73-80
  example of outline for quality control, 72-73

Planning, 71
   and costs, 75
   as element in motivation, 61
   human resources, 74-78
   lesson plan for, 11-12
   material resources, 75, 79-80
   for performance reviews, 102
   philosophy of, 73-74
   steps in, 71
   techniques of, 71-72
Planning period, of organizing, 89
Position write-ups
   purpose of, 91
   sample, 91-97
      quality assurance clerk, 97
      quality assurance technician,. 95-96
      quality control inspector, 96
      quality control manager, 91-92
      quality engineer, 93-94
      senior quality assurance technician, 94-95
   self-exercise in, 97-98
Positive action, 65
Problem, definition of, 51
Problem employee, case study of, 66
Problem solving, 51
   case study, 53-54
   lesson plan for, 10
   and problem prevention, 53
   process of, 51-52
   use of task force, 52-53

Q

Quality assurance clerk, position write-up of, 97
Quality assurance technician, position write-up of, 95-96
Quality control inspector, position write-up of, 96
Quality control manager, position write-up of, 91-92
Quality engineer, position write-up of, 93-94

R

Racial relationships, policy for dealing with, 18
Reading, as form of communication, 42
Reassessment, 127
   self-examination exercise, 127-128
Role playing, use of, in problem solving, 51
Rumors, 42

S

Salary, comparison of, for men and women, 17

Senior quality assurance technician, position write-up of, 94-95
Sexual harassment, policy for dealing with, 18
Signs, as form of communication, 42
Staffing, 99
   sample interview questions, 99-100
Stage setting, 3-4
Stress, 24
Supervisor. *See* Manager.
Survey, use of, in measuring morale, 63

T

Tall organization structure, 90
Task force, use of, in problem solving, 52-53
Team leadership style, 29
Termination of an employee, handling, 65
Theory "X" managers, 59
Theory "Y" managers, 59
Time management, 83
   lesson plan for, 11-12
   management by objectives (MBO), 83-85
Two-way communication, 38-40

U

United States Marine Corps, morale of, 62
Upward communication, 40-41

V

Verbal communication, 41
Visual communication, 42

W

Women
   reasons for working, 17
   salary level of, 17
   in work force, 17
Work force
   composition of, 17
   lesson plan for, 8
   management of, 17-23
   and older workers, 19
   and racial relationships, 18
   and sexual harassment, 18
   and stress, 24
   women in, 17
Written communications, 42